The Irish Annals

Of

New Zealand

By

Michael O'Leary

Earl of Seacliff Art Workshop
Paekakariki 2015

978-1-86942-156-4

1

The man himself, cork in hand, in the way of his incestors PISSIN' it up again' ta wall, agin it all here he is now moving to the left, moving to the right, moving through that dark soul of the night, rocking rhythm of the moving train telling him he cant go home, you cant go back clickety clack, you cant go back clickety clack, down the track he finish his mimi, he opens the door the train lurches forward the train lurches back, himself opens the door with handle by hand bandora's pox (as O'Brien's missus Mrs O'Brien might have said, eh! Mango) zap! wrong door he's gotitt zap eh woowoowoowoo train lurches forward train lurches back unstable on feet too much whiskey and crack himself lurches sideways out on to the...smack! goes the skull by the railway track (skully dooo, skullydooooo) skullydo goes the train into the night from the point where the story ends and begins...its (somewouldsayprobably) a grave matter as the grey matter seepsnotspills out tangiblethoughts steady flowofalifetime and beyond the worstthing is that noone isthere to record these ebbingthoughts as they spill over on to ballastandsleeper a seriousbusiness is a paddyontherailway (the railway in eighteenhundred andfourtyone! the yearafterthistorybegun! but nodoubt there will be some beforeandafter aswell) so the blood was flowin', and the life was goin' and was socold in this socalled centralnorthisland, snow wasfallin' and was turningred aroundhishead and soitgoes, life ebbsandflows...himself's life ebbs as his bloodflows from his mouthand from his nose but what heknows also seepsout and what othersknow also from heresay and heressey and henessey and the manyotherthings which makeup the knowledgeofalifetime and feelings from withinandwithout which travel through the generatinggenerations etangataetangataetangata...itspeople and the worldcan turn withoutit but the people cant...the cold comes through hisbody but he cannotmove and the greymatter seeps on to the greyballast, it is mixed and mingled with the traditional usque baugh and as this wateroflife flows out with greyblood himself is alaughing untilithurts (which is not long) and he lolls and then rolls down the bank crying with laughterandpain he he ha ha he helands in a bush and the usque baugh has gothimthinking untilithurts (which is not long) he is ina Bush with Padraic O'Laoghaire (an old americanmobilecarcarbeepbeep or kaka beakbeak) the firstman (arguably) to make a b i c y c l e in Aotearoa and then a few generators later the firstman to leave $2000 (twothousanddollars) to his cousin upon his tragic butverycath olican dirishmaorideath ofsuperstitiouslove and his cuz spent the money not on a Bush ride but a bus ride A.R.A., I.R.A. drunk with negroes (called Cordon to a man) and driving through suburbs neverdreamed of by Padraicbycle and never again seen by the namesake O'Laoghaire who died in the latterdayarms of his Wahine tobe or (as it turned out) nottobe but now himself sickfrom laughingcrying at this newdimensionof Paddy on the railway had rolledbeyond the point wheretrains could see him perhaps and henow toosick and dying to do...so when he saw the lightdownthetrack and heard the clickettyclack he could only see and hear the train go past him like watching the eyeofgod slipping by another humansoul in the darknight and because heknow hewas beyond influencing the diety (in this case an express goods from Taihape) at the same time O'Laoghaire rode up the mainstreet of Lawrence around 1892 and Padraic died in the alms of Henrietta around 1982 himself started feeling the cold all the more as the usque baugh drained out of his gap...his holeinhishead through which hethought...and its a funnything he thinks that herehe is lyingdying and it seemsthat all he can thinkofis an ancient form of transport as it wheelspast hispast and seems to evoke and invoke the oldones and the oldoldones and the oldoldoldones and the oldoldoldoldones to come and see him atlast and himself lying there in a poolofbloodandslushandsnowfalling...its the ringringring of the thing that hehears and hesees the bike withhismummy riding and she comes and to tell him astory as mummydo...mummysay that shedaddy (he granddy) was in and around Tarawera (the Maori tara no the Irishtara) when theresheblows...she peddleon past saying the Grandda was pushedby he mummy (the Arawa by canoeofbirth) by coincidenceof birth across theearth from nearthe old village to

Tauranga (now a newvillage) ringring shebikes off with only the hint of thingstocome seen in her reflectorlight...himself his tinking or tinkering with oddthoughts he thought, why am I thinking likethis on my white deathbedofsnow 1 know or have known that yourlife flashesbeforeyou when youdie he said fornoone to hear but then the paincame and he was dreamingagain...a trainofthought (an expressionless goodone toldhim tryandbehappy for godisgood no pun ishment intended despite the rumours) was up the line linedup ineach carriage woo woo ring ring its himself thistime passing bybike wavingto himself cockinhand pissing after pissingup large, against the Aoteafuckwitcentre (neverhave somany paidso much for the enjoyment of sofew) leaving abig stain under the plaque laid by the ghostqueen of fuckingengland the bitchwho (twit towoo) twit two pervades our consciousness like an unseen unclean poison posingpoised on ourmoney glossymags andher oldfag old hag (the flag) unionjackinherbox fuckingus still, or as we move still in the grip of motherfuckingen gland ringring brrring brrring and he bi cy cl es away from himself leaving himself lying there with the memories of the sonofpule and the sonofglasgow drinking from the stolen bottle while the raincame and the donner und blitzen both lover and wife crashed andflashed sending the manyheaded moviegoing multitude scattering inall directions from and across Aoteasquare and theylaughing at the follyandwetness of humanity and themselves...he musedat the passionatenature of thatlast blast, prettyvitriolic e boy as he re member if rememberit was he himself (the divided se lf noless) had been writing or tryingto write the Irishhistroy of Newzealandandnowlook at him willyou, anothertrain of tort was on the sidingofhismind, his slidingmind gradually shunting (oozing oooozing woooozing) out like the jampacked blackhole ofcalcutta express (something todo with the universe beginning in that holeyblack indiosincity buthe could neverunder stand SCIENCE ifyou knowwhat theymean) or was it the bigbang or pigpen or bigpain theory youprefer anyway the train pulledout (holy catholiccontraceptive!) holysmoke and himself think ifthink is the word...anywayman twateveritis theres a slowtrain coming like the slowcum trailingaftere jaculation everydrop is beingsquuezedout this willnot bean easydeath...samoansong is coming (sic) along butit is back to Tara where a relative (it's all relative dozensofcousins and all the others are sistersandbrothers) no notyet, nyet, Taranaki nakinakinightmare riding on the night mare, O'Halloran's Light Horse, traitor to the causeofcourse and yet probably driven by thehunger itself, and driven by Titokowaru offshore to be O'Halloran's Light House forever off the coastof Opunake as a flybynight beakon (like a nocturnalbird) the only light in a life ofshadows with thedarkness of stormyskies and the darkness of winternights and finally just the d a r k n e s s itself te po, te po, te ponui...but himself wakes up laughing despite the dark for hehas hada thought, it's madcow disease except that hisbrain has not melted from the inside from eating sheep pelletsbut is melting the snowof the centralplateaux ifit goeson toolong there will be floods! he laughsandlaughs but that's the extent of his actions for he has broken things besides hishead youknow his legs forexample...brrring brrring, rrring, rrring, itsthe paihikara o Aotearoa (etahi?) and onit is Corbett the inspector of insects, incest, ancestors and he's got a storytotell to bring himself downtoearth (as if he could getany closer!) with astory from which Corbett of the ancestor (the othertwo werenot invited for obscure reasons) and it was fitting that heshould arrive on suchtran sport him being re lated (belatedly, although) to the third pirihimana (the unholy trinity as you will) and he, not himself, started the story of the tupuna with a child's haka (anold cancan)..."first three months not feeling verywell, secondthree months mypuku getting sore, thirdthreemonths 1 thought Iwas inhell, gonnabe a hottime in the oldtown tonight...nowlisten to something you dontknow" and himself listen in utter disbelief (could there besome thing he dont know? and it seems that O'Halloran wasa Dark Horse afterall within 3vols and their influence on Stainlesssteel O'Grady andstone guts O'Curry and many other O's OOOOOOOOOO) to Corbettspeak, "you himself, 1 have ontheback back of mybike one of yourown you didnotknow" and helook tosee hisownoldone but sheis youngand giving birthto his greatgrandda dadadadada, should have been in the village of Te Ariki and the goldeneyes of the carvingsare beginning totangi forthey knowwhat is coming and theyknow thatthey are thereason if there isreason, they heard the koreroporangi and theysaw thewakakehua out on the lake and as the tapuchild is born theworld explodes and the terraces, whewhero a ma, and Te Ariki and Te Moura are buried undermudsodeep but your greatgrandda dadadada was bornin Rotorua because of complications so insteadof being entombedalive at birth hewas pushedbypram to Tauranga toescape thedeath until hedied lateron in his life, himself lookaround to see nothing butsnow and blackness and Corbettbicycle, his birthgiving young oldone shehas disappeared like the canoeitself (whowill believe) brrring rrring Corbettsoff...himself leftstunned in his colddeath bedthinking funny oldlife finding out youare Arawa onlyhours before your inevitabledemise...then heremembers something suchas hisresearch es, how hetie twoandtwotogether when accidentallystumble on aquoth from the Maoripake hahaha of 1873 thus "I have nothing to report except thatif allyour schools are goingon aswellas thatof Wirinake therewill soonbe no Maori in newzealand," atfirst hethought this tobe iron icalor satyr ical but thenon secondthought, not! Here member rela ting thistothat quoth from the chance ellor of the ex chequer of En gland that the penal laws of 1704 demon strated "thatthe system didnotpresume an Irishcatholic toexist except for the purposeof punishment" (nopun!)...hisbrain wasreeling as the realpolitik ofhis peoplesenemy wasre vealed, so that he existed despite the hopedfor passive (butat times brutal) attempted genocide of the Irish and Maori people wasnot just paranoia or conjecture but as realas the gasovens except theydidn't have the technology until itwas toolate and he fellas leep as theblood of thesetwo peoples pulsedthrough him and also drainedout of him...there's nojustice, there's just us, helaught at theab surdity of language asa way of trying to understand thisworld suddenlyhe wantsto laughand singand danceand drink, drink, drink with anebulous goal tofind the limitlessmind and soul, lifeis movement andhe cant move, for the sake of his forsaken ancestors he is noa! and his invisability is painful...hea woke to the whispering wires of the electrictrains whichnow runbe tween Te Rapa and Palmerston North in the south and asthe lightshone on the tracksabove him hetried desperately to move his dogsbody to aposition wherehe might beseen but despite his great agitation he was toofar down the bank for any enginedriver tosee anymore than a brief swaying ofa a dark shadowbush against the whitenight snow ifile saw anythingat all, atall, attall, and the click-clack of the wagonsgoing over eachsleeper made himselffeel soalone that hesimply cried and cried...rrring rrring fuckoff bbrring bbrrring fuckoff hedont want anymore bicycles but still its brrring rrring it's Mango O'Brien with a book and an aiitu ridingon the back of te paihikara...samoan song Samoansong O'Brien whispers softly and places the openboo k spook infro nt of himse elf...it's anold diary and while himself strains and struggles toreadit O'Brrrringbrrringbrien and the aiitu leavehim to it...heread "25.12.45 Berlin, thisday iscold andit isa daywhich haunts (saynothing of witch hunts) meeveryyearof my life andwill until Idie. Herein Berlin things are badbut practical. Wekeepalookout for looters (all kout forloo ters) and black marketeers andcheck peoplespapers fornazis whoareon theloose using forgeddocuments allfairlyroutine andits usu allyonly the smallfish who getcaught...but evenseeing those bastards, having liberatedafew of the deathcamps earlierthisy ear (especially Buchenwald) eventhis and the terrible memoriesof those corpses deadand alivepiled ontopof each other asthe SS exited, eventhis did notstir imne the angerand incomprehension Ifeeland havefelt for thelast (16) sixteeny ears...fearguilt self loathingbut mostofall anger andincom prehensionare what 1 havelived with since the (28) twentyeight of (12) december 1929 theday Idiscovered evilin the world andin myself (blacksaturday) and caused theseparation from theworld, fromgod, but mostof all fromher ...Melisia, howlhave saidyour nameten derly andsoft lyand lovingly whenwe laytogether orin sadnessas I face the lonelinessof life w i t h o u t you...itseems likei am destined to shootyour ancestors bothliving anddead until i dieandbeyond...Ihave beenshoo ting germansnow for sixyears (andyou wereof germanandsamoanblood) itslike beingin hell where ikeep killinyou and ourlove for eternity...mumsent afew things from homethe otherday andamongthemwas aphoto ofmelisia takenjust before i lastsaw her"...himself wasfilled with heart-break ashe readthis luminated manuscript, ithad been written witha penthat made it slightlyglow in the dark, alsothe snowhad stopped fallingand te marama came out from behind her veilso that hecould just readwhat hehad read andnomore buthim self was facinated bythis diaryspeci ally seeing that during this break enforced by his sorehands needing a break (they werealreadybroken) helook edat who wroteit and saw ithad been his ownfather who haddied heknew ofan illness probablynottoolong after thewar...himself settle himself trying topack snow aroundhis hands to numb them from the pain of the fall and whenhe putthe bookin position he read on "29.12.45 Imust write thisdown beforewe goon duty, I dreamedabout Melisia lastnight, Iwas inher village of Foalalo andmy hometownof Hokitika itwasa beautiful day andwe hadntseen eachother for a long time...suddenlyan afakasi child (probably the one we would have had ifwehad) ofa bout fourteen (14) years camerunning sayingyouwereill andhad called myname we ranto the hospitaland youlookedso sick, allyour hair hadgone but I wentover and kissedyou and itwas you and itwasme! Yousaid myname and Isaid yourname and itwas us! I nolonger felt divi dedor cutoff, we wereone andour childwho Ihad neverseen lookedhappy...when I awoke with thefirst lightof thecold germ anwinter just breakingthenight youcame to me and I thought you were reallythere...in the dreamwe kissed andkissed andkissed likewe used to" now It would havebeen himself orat leastpart of him self hadhe beenborn during thatlove be tween his father and Melisia during his fat hers tourof duty in 1920s Samoa, hewas thinking howwhen he was young heused tothink abouthow hewould have been different (orwhetherornothewouldhave) ifhe had beencon ceived afewyears earlier orlater than hewas or if he hadhad a different motherorfather than his fatherormother andnow here wasa tangible tangello ofan experience of justthat eventhough ithad beenjusta dreamhis father hadhadhadhadhadhadhahahaha he he he he hereadon..."later inthe eve ning

29.12.45, I shotsome one todayfor loo ting shoo ton sight are ourorders. Its strange amongthese ruins where somany people havedied, thatone moreperson shouldmake any difference youget usedtokilling inan abstractsort of way, but deepdown you neverdo. The moment I shot this man, I hearda terriblewail (not unlike oldahab) andthen smallercrys of papapapapapa I lookeda round andjust to the rightof me in the doorway ofa bombedout banka woman and two kinder appeared who wered ressedin DresdenBlackrags and looked verystark and desolateandthin against the greyhalfbuildings and thesnow which was fallingheavily theyall cametowards me and the woman shouted somethingatmeingerman and then threw herselfontopof the corpsecrying. The children stoodbeside their parents silentandfrightened lookingat me with sadeyes afterawhile the Motherunfolded the handwiththestolenobject; init was aloafof mouldybread which shegave to her children who ateitravenously. I thoughtof Melisia and her children (ifshehadany) I went roundthe cornerandvomitted andcriedandcriedandcried until I fellto the ground withexhaustion. I felt like a mogamoga something which has existed since the beginning of time and hasa hardshell and fullof whitepus inside...I comebackbackbackbackto (nonotthetraintotimbuckto) barracks and I started thinking about that blacksaturday in Apia and Ican still seeher brother Mani whohated thefact of hissister going witha palagi (andespecially a NewZealandsoldier because hewas with the Mau) hehad causedall the trouble in their aiga for us so that in the heatofthe shootingwhile watsonslewis was gunning the maumen (Samoamosamoamosamoa) 1 took deliberateaim andbecause Mani fell rightnext to Tupua Tamasese nooneeverknew that there hadbeen a deliberatemurder in ifi'ifi road that day of 28.12.29...itwas wellhidden among the panicmurders of twentynine innocent Samoan protesters whoonly wanted torule their owncountry...it had beenso easy and yetit was the end for meand Melisia. I could neverface heragainand applied forimmediate transfer but I stayed in the army back in New Zealand, when the warcameiwaspleased to beable to shoot people who 1 had noconnection with for I thought I could atone for the death of Mani which worked well rightup to today 29.12.45 when I shot amanfor aloaf (I started out by shooting for alofa and ended up shootingfor a loaf) its all over"...so that's whydad was in the looooooonybin afterthe war, wherehedied himselfthink but cannot say fornow the snow isfalling moreagain heavily thanbefore andhe cannot readanymore not that thereis anymoretoreadanyway...hedreams anddreams an invertedlegend o le tala ia Salevao, Salevaosalevao isfrom Ualotu and Fuluuaalefanua, he is theirchild who was addicted to pigeonsnaring and his othemameis Mataulufotu himselfdreams the wrongwayround as Salevao plays withthe aiitu Mose and had caught many of the birds but couldnot carrythemallso he he he he he ha ha ha has to then ask a groupof travellers ifhe canleave them at Sataura but they chasehim away, sohe creptback and asked anoldlady if he can leavehis birds andshe saysyes...himself is sleeping dreaming as the travellers souls leavetheirbodies and himselfsees that the travellersreallyrepresent the Mau when the Sataua people (who in dream are the Samoans) await their travellingvisitors and fallas leep; But when the oldwoman went to wakethem theywere all dead and himself wakeup afraid and then realising why during his research he found areference to the samoans as theirishofthesouthpacific...brrring brring rrring rrring Melisiarideup witha child onthe backof herbicycle (the same bicyclemade by Padraic oflawrence) she pickup thediary of her lover himself senior shelook athimself and smile sadly (she is beautiful and young like 1929) she says softly "Faa Soifua" and with afakasi shepedals off towards Foalalo...almost immediately the bicyclesback brrring brrring rrring rrrring tingalingtingalingtingaling

a ling is a thing

without a wing

they serve to you on a dish

a thing with a wing

is not called a ling

but is called a flying fish

(or a bird)

then offrides the little poeticpeon, a hapuka noless, nolegs but frontfins guiding the handlebars as the taildivides from the seatand each tipofthetail reaches thepedals hapukaheoff hellbent, like a womanusedtoneedaman towards memoirs, memories and other memorableexperience, let me be frank, includingmemorabilia hangingon ta wall by da bal etc etc ect ect tec tec cet cet cet cte cte tce tec etc etc andall tingalingaling brring rrrring...himself is nownearlyhalfcoveredin snow hestill cannotirnove henogo butagain snowfall stopsfalling to give a momentaryrespite, as theysay, and hisniind is now asclear as the coldnight air and hewaits to hearor eventhink hehear thesound of anothertrain hecan hear the strainofa diesel inpain (ifa dieselfeltpain) asit pulls throughacutting upto the plain (or plateaux somemaybesayn) but thenagain its the mashingofgrain whirlingroundin his brain (ifthats whatyou call suchan insane oreven innane collection of squashed and puffypieces of . . .) but no it reallyis adiesel pulledtrain the relentless hammering of its engine pounding in hishead and he realises that the northandsouthbound expresses have crossed, have made their nightly exchange of peopleandsupplies and nowcontinue ontheirways southandnorth and as the trainpasses himonly metresaway hethinks (andfeels) that this will behis last contact withhis fellowhumanbeings except perhaps for the oddelectricdriver whomayget pass . . .

he is lonely

gonna die

he is looooooonley

gonna die

if heaint deadalready

girlorgodknowsthereasonwhy...ageona electric train eclectrialrain booboobalbaba bafoureyedcuntbut a teacher nun the less in Connemara, inconnemarakickthebecket...and he's brain out like ozone thought the ooozoingzone layer and allof us are underthreat so they wouldhaveusbelieve asif we werentany way andwhere itsgonnaend godonly knowsdownallthe daze...a tribute nearlyashame...a tribunal finds infavourof the landlord because inthe ulti mate endmate heowns the place and thats whatmatters in thisanglofuckensaxon setup...a real set up it is, set up the pieces again after the checkmateeven though you've given hima chequemate and you've allways paidontime (moreorless) and aftersixandahalfyears (61/2) you still haveno rights and after sixandahalf centuries (61/2) theystillhaveno rights andits the same struggle call them bandits (the I.R.A.) outlaw them hangthemall, hangitall, theres no justice, there's just us! So the young irishofthesouthpacific and others use the machette gang where they can to express what they cantexpress bybadjudgeofcharacterofjudges . . .

tis well I do remember

thebleaknovember day

theballiffandtheland

to driveus allaway

theyset the roofon firewith

their cursed englishspleen

and thats the cruelreason

I left old...the songfloated

errily through the holeinthe head having spun round his wholehead and then the verse of realunderstanding was going adding to hisown under standingof the kind of . . .

 now motherdear

godresthersoul

layon the snowingground

shefainted in her languishing

seeing thedesolation round

shenever rose

but passedaway

fromlife to iminortaldreams

and thats anotherreason

I leftold...the kind of historical standoff, sometimes hysterical and nowherehewas himself lying on the samesnowyground sixandahalf (61/2) generations and twelvethousand milesaway, but the manofthe song circa 1840s the nopotatoe song the nopapatoetoe song, not at that point, hewould have laid thousands of miles of railway track (61/2 + 61/2 = 13 - 1 =12 or thereabouts) andhe already had experience onthe Edinburgh (the Dunedinofthenorth) to Howickline...at Corebridgepub the Irishnavvies werepaid and himself's greatgreat greatgreat greatoldone was among themangry anddrunkand wanting to beback home in the southoferin, where hisown sweet Kathleen was having their childasin the songabove, butonly that wasa fewyears later whenthe praitties failed but the cornlaws didnt, but strengthened, but now it is 1846 and paddyis on the railway, therailway just southof edin burgh but notsofar south asto be mixed with the scotsandenglish, notyet nyet atleast, but at Corebridge where the packmanwas of the disapearing watches what watches asked padddy, in this case himselfs oldoldoldoldoldgreatone whos wife was to languish in the snowonlytwoyears later and then himself six anda half (61/2) generations laterin the centralnorthislandplateaux snowofaotearoa...hukatearoa...but nowits at the bridge of gore and blood and the gang of drunken Irish (haurangi = Irish) went to the Constableschristiebrown to free their comarades from prisoncells (brownandchristie) ablow to theirarms and the navvies rip the doorrightoff its hinges...but notforlong didthe peacelastas the scotsandenglish comedown the line forrevenge (utu o te rarewe) joined by Marquis of Lothians colliers at Newbattle inorder (outoforder) to starta new battle...so it was 1,500 against 200 (twohundred against onethousand five hundred toput it anotherway) and the Irish always being adeptat gambling, ran! asthe anglobabarbarourousscots camedown like workerson the fold, and the nextmorning the scottishherald reported "it was trulypit iable to see severalwives of the Irish labourers sittingat shortdistance from the blazinghuts in themidst of afewarticles of fumiturein the cloaks peculiar totheircountry and watchingwith melancholycountenancy the gradualdemolition of their humbledwellings"...while the other navvies gradually hadto make their waybackto camp andpickup the pi ec es this tipuna of himself keptup the run back to Cork wherehe sailedfor and where hisown Kathleen waited for himto return with the richesofthesong...but for all that ive seenhere I mightas well be...and from the Cork hemade his way back to Leap whereshe waited in their desolate cottage (but it was home) not farfrom Skibbereenofthesong...twas here atleap that theystayed, he Patrick Fitzgerald (and Gerald Fitzpatrick if you're thatway) and hiskathleen who hadbeen his colleen and their twobabes wherethey eekededout anexistence for a couple of years (wellat leastenough to paythe landlordenough to stop the everthreatened eviction) until the faminecame and they could neither eek nor eat anymore

she never rose

but passedaway

fromlife

to immortaldreams . . .

she kathleen and she clare (their beautiful andloved fiveyearold daughter) perished innopotatoe snow and stoneygrounds (notunlike the centralnorthisland where mokopuna himself struggled to stayalive against the cold and odds)...so the old onepicked up theremaining youngone (whoin time wouldbe come anoldone him self) and togetherthey leffleap in the deadof nightunseen...and himself in the dead of nightunseen by the NIMT, the nimtline asit were, was stilltinkin' and still whathe wastinkin' wasstill graduallyleaving the mightyhead, red, but not forgreener pastures but forwhiterones...so the quantumleap from Leap, from the landof the long barrenground to the landof the longwhitecloud took place and twomore fitzgeralds with mouthstofeed arrived in N.Z. around 1852 howabout you...and will youtell me now whatsthe difference between an Irishpig anda Polishpig, ashure thatsaisy an anglosaxonpig andits correct aftar onlytwo previousattempts towit, a germanpig and anenlishpig both ofwhich are alsocorrect in their ownway if youcan seeit, but they are even more on the sideof correctness when they are standingtogether at ther samegate dont ya tinkso there Michael, ai I do will yahave anotherpaddy, Oh ai 1 will tanksvery much...the eviction of the ancestor whonow wandered lonelyin thecrowd withonly the company of hisbabe and the sorrow of his deadcolleen haunting him accrossthe barren land as the bansheehowls andhe tries to sleepin the nightly bogholes dugdaily and coveredby the turf...in the rushto killat Kilrush William Butler notyet Yeats nyet wrote and 1 quoteofa tumbling hesaw with twelveyearold eyes...(atumbling of the tippswho would laterappear in the centralotago fieldof goldin competition withthe Chinese butthats another story as you will findout..."Thesherrif, a strongforce ofpolice and aboveall the crowbarbrigade, a body composedof the lowest andmost debauchedruffians werepresent...signalfrom the sherrif the miserable inmatesof thecabins were draggedout, thatchedroofs were torndown, earthenwalls battered inby crow bars (where crows hangout), screamingwomen, halfnakedchildren, paralysedgrandmother and totteringgrand da were hauledout," (all this caused by thehalfacre clause and the £4 clause Russellspolicy based onthe courseof Englishbenevolence being frozen by insultculmuny and rebellionand a few other thingsto boot) Butlerwenton, "I thinkif a loadedgunhad been putinmy handsat the time 1 wouldhave...the winterof 1848-49 dwells in my memory as onelongnight of sorrow"...andso it waswith the Patrickfitzgerald who nowheaded for whatheknewnot, butwhichwouldbe Aotearoa...Brrrrrum brrrrrum vrooomm vrroooomm if itisn't the V8 pushbike (not B4 time although originallymaybe) and ifit isn't Pita Edith (worldfamous innewzealand) one Olds thistime notan oldone as before (not B4) andhimself quiteovercome with an ocean of the thoughts (the torts to remaininside thelaw!) as his memoryglands secrete secretly...pitaedit h looksdown on the creaturehimself and takes pity edits the latest sentence ofhimself who thensees the tripodseat on the veeeight tricycle with the stamp MAD (E) IN PARIMOANA OF ORIGIN OREGEN, PINE FOR PAST etc and him selfcan only thinkonething...te nohoanga o te porangi...pitaedith wholooks off ended has turnedinto Edithpiaf but b 44 (and not B4) before himself can sayany thing shehe cycles off singinga song of thehi story of the V8 called...PSYCLES and himself catches snatches..."smooth geared underpants raiders / in '39 they tested the first VI by '43 your owners had turned to genocide / gallonsof legalgas were dishedup / and the V2 smashed into your stretched / marks theynearly broke the deutchebanks as the riversofmoneyflowed and thepeople you degraded thought itsa goodthing thegermans neverinvented the V8, the VI andV2 werebadenbadenenough but you movedalong narrowroads dreamingof the nazisparty"...and as the last strains of thissadreframe echoed through the snowcovered landscape himself couldnt helpthinking itstill alongway to Tipperary and travellin' all those Miles, no Gasoline, so intothe petroltank a gallon of poteen andit wentlike abomb ifyou know what 1 mean all theway from Tipperaryto youknowwhere I mean soit stoppedjust - short of St Stephensgreen and toall of thepeople who saidwhere youbeenthe drivingman replied blessed arethose whobelieveand havenot seen theyr'e killing menandwomen for the wearingofthegreen but now I mustgo backto where I'vebeen andhe pulledout the bottleofpoteen anddrinks halfhimself sothathe eyesareagleam, thenhe pouredtherest into hismachine and all the plainpeople of Ireland cando isstare at the wonderofitall...beep beep, burp burp...but him selfas waspredicted issoon laughingon theother side ofhisface (myboy!) because notinthe toodistant distance he sees the twosistersriding in tandem ona tandem (daisydaisy I'm half crazy!) their seductive soft rrring rrrring rrrring is heard and his dingaling responds naturally, naturally - heloves andwants themboth, their broth has beensimmering on hisfire for manymoons and as they appear fromout of the darkness the snowstopsfalling and themoon againappears brightand full inthe coolrnid winter sky and as the sisters pull nearerto this neredogood both of themsilently (forthey donotspeak to oneanother) dismount (sic) and hecan see thepeak of the centralnorthisland mountains rising everhigher before him and as te marama (whois alsoone ofthe sisters) andher starspiked cloak spreadover him hefeels theancient volcanoes which are above himand beneath himand around him, they are also withinhim and the centuriesold lavabetween hisloins beginsto move, heisenchanted and embraced by her nakedness which is underher cloak foronly him tosee butjust as theyare aboutto reach hispeakof their lovemaking heforlornly lookson as theother sister pushes Marama to oneside of him andas theybegin a jealous and maliciousfight he, himself, sees himselfas Pihanga and the twosisters are Tongariro and Taranaki fightingover thesameman who in legendwasa woman andthey weremen andas hesees te atahua o te marama recedingfrom him to the west he sees thatshe was themother of hisdaughter (not his daughter) andhe is fullof sadness forher return buthe hasno time to think forthe victorious wahine o te Tongariro isonto him, andhe is helplessas she winds herwebb of seduction aroundhim her beautiful brownbreasts are delicately and deliciouslyabove him andhe feels her teke opening onto his fully erect raho andshe is moving inlong slow gestures herface ecstatic in the moonlight, histouch and hertouch sosensuous they both ache andcryout together andthrough his ears atsmall intervalshe hears her whisper almost inaudibly "comein, comein" inurgent shortburstsof hervoice, and then "letit stand" (as a tilt of the hat to the master) as the onlyunbroken partsof his bodyrespondsto her invocations hermouth hungry yetsubtle findshis, herthick firmsoft lips meet hisand theirtongues entwine asthey kissandfuck kissandfuck kissandfuck and she comesbefore hedoes in moansand groans of pleasure and release andjust as the earthshakes andhe isabout toerrupt, hiseyes closed in semiconscious sweetness of sweat and the smells of sex scenting the coldair, hehears brring brring and hiseyes open to seetwo sisters ridingoff ontandem, and as he sees Marama fold hercloak of stars around her hesees their daughter, Moana alsodisappear, and Hine whohas come hasnow gone also, the three of them rideoff intandem as they abandon himself lying there, theone one part of hisbody left standing silhouetted against the fallingagain snow and hisbody writhes in sexualagony which hecant evenrelieve because evenhis fingers arebroken...(itsa hard life!)...and as the strengthof his sex ualdesire gradually dissipates heis left feeling drainedand bereft with morepain becauseof the further bruises andcuts hegot, he begat during his dreamreality of begatting, heis melancholyalso from hispost coital non coitusmetionedout andits notjust his grey which matteroffactedly oozes as he loses more as time goesby, playwith it again Hine hecalls andwishes andwants as hissperm also oozesout onto the whiteness of virginsnow but he is ofcourse alone (there is doubtwhether even mandrakes willgrow in thisclimate!) well I'll be hanged (orwell hung asit might havebeen back in 1984 old hat now, and nowhere tohangit - put it in the hangi and we'll seehowit comes out kapai te kai) and ashis manhood drainsaway sodoes hislife and hisbrain stilloozes onto this page as the paincomes inwaves comesinwaves comesinwaves lappingat thefeet of his (himselfs) existence, the thoughts and the pain becomeone as theyreach across the sea ofhis existence from eternity, the ancestors are calling and coming, hislovers are calling and his children (not his children) are callingand coming, hisparents are calling and coming his sistersand brothers and manyothers arecallingand coming, those whohave neverbefore seen him are callingandcoming callingandcoming callingandcoming like an ancient karanga calling the mokopuna home this callingandcoming is pullingat hislife but he resists hewants to live hewants to survive hewantsto see his children (not his children) grow. Hewants warmth andcomfort and love, not these maddelusions andinsights let himwalk down the street andfeel the ground and see the coloursoflife not this black andwhite landscape of unrelenting coldness and loneliness inwhich his lifeis gradually receding even the whiskeywarmth is beginning to wane (Jesus wane whereis Jesus) as it too oozes its finite fulfullness slipping the everwidening gap he is dying throughahole inhishead...soitseems factsmustbe faced...thinking only keepsout the ghosts like the daykeeps out thenight...himself hearsthe whistle of alongago train andthinks fora moment thathe mightbe saved, butagain its onlya memoryof whatused tobe tiedto a hopeof what mighthavebeen, if you knowwhat Imean, Imean Imean Imean andwhat Imeanis, andwhat himself hearis, anold song, an air floatingon the air comingacross the wavesfrom Galwaybay, ofthe lossof the railcar from Finn Valley (Donnegal) as the lossofthe railcarfrom Palmerston (Otago), himself listens. . .

Oh, someday I'llgo backagain to Seacliff (Glenties)

 itmaybe at the closingof theline (tolocalpassengers)

to see thesun riseover Puketeraki (Achla)

and themoon beamson Blueskinbay (Gweebarra) softlys

thelorries now bringup ourfittle rations

the buses seldomhalt wherewe wouldgo (the coastroad)

for we whofive inglensand mistyvalleys

speaka language thatthose Wellington (6 county) ladsdontknow

when I'mfarawayfrom Evansdale (Finntown) andfrom Seacliff (Glenties)

Idreamofwhen I'll seethose glensagain

butit breaksmy heart when Iremember

theoiddays when 1 travelledby the train

I see herstandingstill waitingat Port Chalmers (Strandar)

1 hearher whistling into Sawyers Bay (Ballybofey)

The oldfolk speaking Maori (Irish) upat Waikouaiti (Cloghan)

And the littlecottage lightsalong the way

ashe listens he sees thetime the oldone spent working on the line of the abovesong of O'Kelly and O'Laoghaire the calfkeeper's grandson, and was workingon it when the moneyand drive carried the line further southfrom Newtownstewart to Omagh, whichwas reachedin 1852, but then the potatoe was a gain not there (no grain eitheragain) and a train of thoughts passedby carrying more statistics than people for the countydonegal ie.

pop: 1841 = 296,000

pop: 1851 = 255,000

pop: 1861 = 237,000

pop: 1951 = 180,000

sos that having lept from Leap the oldone (or oldoldoldold one to be pedantic) popped up briefly in the 1851 Donegal pop:, but by 1861 he had popped off to Aotearoa and was workingon getting ajob on another narrowgaugerailway twelvethousand milesaway whichis notbad going, thought himself to himself withpride, the knowledge of his ancestor laying 12 thousandmiles of railway inonly 10 years made himfeel fullof warmth and he almost could sense the snowandice melting around him suchwas his sensibility...but the reality wasdifferent forboth and as the statistictrain rolled away down the line ofhistory woe woe woooe woooe he could feel the melancholy of his race with its fullweight upon...up on himmmmm...and anotherdrift of snow blew across the barren wasteland, hewas the stuffed man (really tired), he wasthe hollowman (hollowhollow - anybodyhome?) his headpiece wassurrounded by hoarfrost and the deep whiteness threatened to en gulf him en tire ly...so Patrickfitzgerald stepped off the donegalrailway in eighteenfiftytwo and sailed with his nowgrowing child far andtheywere wellat sea (although there were manywho were not wellof course, there weresome who were welloffcourse!) when he realised he and his littleone wouldbe landingin New Zealand and not New York (what do youmean not New York!) and he just thought, hunger doesfunny things to a man (but as an afterthought, not so funnythings to a woman, as he remembered his wife like an old sackof spuds lying on the frozen Irish ground and he crydandcryd)...things startedto slow, the lifeflow even the snow fell oneflake ata time, sweetjesus and eve ry word, eve ry thought broke up in to syl a bills fal ling down and down through his mind, through the con sci ous ness of him self and his im pond er able sit u a ti on and his im poss ib le pre dic a mant (but not sta ted) the word s be came less com pre hen sib le the (or though) hard er he tried to un der stand, he felt that his brain (ourbryanee) was a slow ly spin ning spin oze an fish tank (anunderwandawll) and nev ere societ why of disc boy lik eee in snoweee rivets of cru mpie gup gup gup as trang erbel ieve dubble seaing hap pap me weep on sun day mass des truction tra ction yip sno sno sno fal fal fal the wo man eyem tink ingov the lifeflow even the snow fell oneflake ata time, sweetjesus and eve ry word, eve ry thou oght broke up in to silly bus a bills fal ling down and down through his mind, through the con sci ous holes ne us of him self and his im pond er able in sit u a ti on and his im poss ib le pre dic a mant (but not sta ted) the word s be cume loss com pre hen syb le the (or though) hard er he tried to kun der stand, he felt that his bain (ourbryanee) was a slow ly spint ing sprig ooze an fish tank (anunderwandawll) and nev ere societ why of disc boy lik eee in snoweee rivets of cru mpie hulup gup gup as trang erbel ieve dubble seaing hap pap me of you boat fame, and if onelooked close by e nough (iseoughisenough) oughts like flick er ring sparks wereing or gent lyspin ning out of his nose...bleed

but	gent ly		broth her	gent	ly underst andand	
this		slow	p ro	cess	is one	
of	the	un	col	lect	ed	tho ughts andwo and
rds	and	dis	eas	es	of	theman himself
passed		on	un		hind	dered
as	the	snow		fell	light ly	and was
whirl	ed	a		round and	kept	from
settlingby amo unt ain						
of	wind	whichhad		sprungup		but	now itis
justas (no		there	is		none) jesusjester	
qu icklyand	quietlybeg an t ofall and					
the	snowandthe	WO	rds began			
flowin g		MO	refreely		againsoso	
tha	t	him	self	wasyet	again	trying toregain to gain
respitefrom burialby w hitearth (nothownow						
cow	boy,	not	the	cow!) . . .		
tokeep		warm		if	only	internally,he thought he

of his wife (not hiswife) and he tried to compose the most beau tiful poem in the world to her, whichwas something he had al wayswanted todo for her, he thought and randomlines from pastpoems he had written toher sauntered through as someonestood lookingat the starlitsky dreaming, titiro ki te tonga saw the pot and scorpions tale (but didnt listen to the noise of the chuggingdiesel engine saying whakarongo mai her last words till next time my darling goodnight) whakarongomai through te po o te pari moana...but that was someoneelse for the snowfell on himself in the measuredmetre of blankverse...he longed to give expression to the passionhe felt forher, sometimes so strong he felt the skywould open and the universe wouldexplode through eternity but he wascalm as the words flowed, old words he wanted towrite newones but the old ones pushed out and fell through his consciousness with the samesteady consistency withwhich the snowfell...slowlycreeping nga kupu atahua, nga kupu o te aroha, nga kupu ora, nga kupu o te mate, forward they came one by one, the words of the past, moving through the present towards the future, then to linkupagain with the past (the point of misunderstanding for the anglosaxonfuturists)...whakarongo! we satsilent at the footof the poetsstatue...we waited...for the time wewould nolongerbe to gether...myarm moved instinctively a way...we are a part wegrowtogether...the aroha is be tweenus as well as the dis tance...thebestthing was we were happy...we laughed and danced sang...and talked of death and darkness and light...to sitsilent at the foot of the poets statue...kia aroha, kia kaha e wahine toa!...one thousand miles is not a long distance for dreams to travel, unravel as the mystery grows...the evil and the joy of the world are within all of us...storms of destruction and devastation standalong side the beauty of the sky meeting the sea at the horizon, the gently blowing wind scattering the small whispyclouds, the headland juts out its ancient form and manyvarieties of trees transform the latewinter landscape with their colours and shapes reaching upandout wards, the sea seems lifted above the land, reaching and meeting the heavens half way...brrm brrm, rrring rrring rrring the peace fulpoe tic scene of wordandsnow was suddenlyshattered by ifit isnt pitaedith backa gain riding shotgunwedding on the back ofa Harley and at the apehangers steering and heering and swearing is her boy friendfrom the notorious patch honki toothfairy (himselfthink always think edith wasa way with the fairies)...they roarup and stop, honki takes a swipeandaswig, he has tattooed on his forehead "tobe or not tobe is hard for the people," thus indicat ing he is a member of the literary mob...he hands the bottle of whiskey toedith and himself catches the faintly the words "i roto i te koraha pore kau he potae" (himself the remembers the blightplight ofhis ownones who cameto him with the story of beingin the wilderness without a potatoe and he laughsandcries) honkicomes over to himself and pours a large draught of the water oflife down his throat it is all he cando, "Gottago bro, you just like us, e, laughing and crying at the same time, kia ora begorrah e hoa haere ra!" hehops on the bike andtheyreoff, and as the soulsoothing whiskey permeates thebody of himself every cell in his body is resurrected from death and soned at the sametime the living is easy, fishyjumping brrm brrring brrring brrring honkiedith off towards where the sunset would be if it wasnt aftermid night "we gonnalet it allhang out" are the last things he hears with ears...con fusion...arthurormathur...the poemere turn, but now dis join ted...his head swims from brainawashwithwhiskey...as unchained manacles release chained limbs...the manu o aroha was about to express its new freedom...the penis mightier than the words butboth areof course connected to love and words lastlonger...army Amagh 1 hope the little ladycomes by whatever method (I got rhythm) "there's noloving onlyfucking" orat least Sam thinks before hekicked that becket agin but shehas otherideas 1 daresay from heresay or should I sayas I heard hersay before I kissed her goodnight as passionately as circum stances allowed...and now I dream andwait and its the greatmind of himself, te wahi moemoea of herself and he can see his mind is begin ningtogo as hesees her and her sister and her sister's sister and hersister's sister's sister and soon until there are twentyorso in arow like an arrow atahua tatou and heknows his mind follows from nowon the ancient celticsym bols (inspect her) from the book of Kelly's whose whirlpools and whirlwinds weave and wind from within and without in continuous travelfingand unravelling of knowledge and understanding now lost nowgained, the kellywho brought it from Dub was Lynn (new and grey for that matter) the darklin of the formerlin and then the lin of the latter getting darkerstill as time goesby you must remember this, and the old mind infuses the air like a karanga influences the ear which hears...aline is drawn alongwhich travels the thoughts and feelings falling and failings of a generation butit is not the straightline of historical accuracy...itis the mystery enveloping (no prizes for guessing what)...but, himself, looks up tosee the oldwoman whocomes walking pushinga bike uphill and shesees himself lying there and is happy to have someoneto talkto...shelays her girisbike down and starts "Are youa Cataholic now?" he noreplies (happened oncebefore) and soshee (bar but not banshee yet noone screeching night mareily across the barren wastelandyet) asksa gain "Are youa Cataholic, then?" thennow the savage nowthen reply of himself (in his mind, off course) "Well, 1 like cats, especially blackpussey, yes but I'm no fan attic," and she, who hassettled in says "well I'm not talkinga bout supersitition but religion" and he "samedifference" answersing face eatiously (what mouth whatamouth) she lookshurt but explains to hisquest ioning that she has alpineclimbers disease and is forced to wanderin the heights for the restof her days and nights, no rest for the whickers or any other baskets from the Blaskets or whereabout, so shesays would youlike a ga me of Spoil Five and pullsout the pack of cards...I cannot play sayshe (himself)...just listen, she explains, highest ina redsuit, lowestin a blacksuit, takes the trick...two of spades beats anyten, except diamonds...knave of the ownsuit, trump beats kingand queen...but the five of the suitbeats alleven the jack...aceof hearts has specialpowers canbe beaten but trumpace, knavefive can cross suits! playedfora pool eachrounds...object to stop others winning!...I cannot play himself re it er ates, somehow point ingto his mangled hands "Oh," she says "Well I'd bettergo, I'll tellyou this" andhe listens to Moi, no Rita by the metre made, tell herstory to his...its like she's not there at all, it's like sheishim, like hermad ness has mingledwith his, so what sheisaying is coming from inside his head...being the last of myfaminerly and not livingin mynative land I williamtell of things that apple between myeyes other wisewould belost forall times...succeeding generations mayask whoam I, wheredid I comefrom...by this I hope Iwill beable to help those see their pre deces sors against the back dropof lifeasit wasin Ireland in those days, the people whogave them faith, loveof Ireland andits culture through the upsand downs of the troubledpast, we've had toem igrate becauseof the existing con ditionsin Ireland which brought bus iness and trains toa standstill...what was knownas the Suezcrisis finallyde feated us aswe owneda garagein Chapelzod, the pig bigoil comp anies swallowed and swilled the small bus inesses by curt ailing petrol under theguise of short ages, whenin fact the oiltankers were fullout side Dublin Bay...wewentto Ballyshannon to say fare well to our loved ones (there was a waugh on!) a heart breaking experience and when we got to Newzealand...at this point Rita pointing to points' north said she must begoing forshe had morealpines to climb and as she headed northandsouth, eastandwest pushingher little bike dearold tyke had she beena child it wouldhave been a trike whichit was because shewas...I have more stories shecalled backtohim (shecalledbacktohymn) and himself could hear the turaluratingalingling of herbell (or) and he wasa lone but not for long (not Fellong your working for is it Joseph, notforlong) nolonger than a furlong away as the duck flies or the riverruns past no itsnot green, see, its or time flows or rooffloors, or opendoors, anywaywhat should happen but didn't the sky openand the cloudsparted and a loathsome noise some miles away heard from a ????? the earland the Banshee crys????? wailing songs and see, shanties and ballads and the like, singing deathsheads sheepskulls spinning and the terrifying gigglingwhirl all the while as the lightning flashes but is unheardof because of the miles away which it is out over the seeto the east (andjuliet is the son?)...te marama reveals herself from behind her cloudyvale, showlight enough for life, not for love...the earland the Banshee went to town wrappedup ina brown paper train, and never came home again...whirlygigs and gigglywhirls serves you right you gigglygirls, ticaloon on a lunatic world one, two, three nowtwirl...and suddenly the sky burst open through a hole in a largelightning flash and fourlargefingers and onelargethumb, the hand of God noless, came down and plucked himself from the cold desolate earth and transported him Deus ex machine...

2

...Deus ex machina shelanded, the little nun (answer to the ancientquestion, whatfun do monkshave) Sister Mary Himself, topshelf, heresto your health, she sneakedinto latermasslate and onlyby stealth wasun detected, delectable though shemay havebeen had shenot sworn to have worn habbits which meant she hadbits which you wouldn't haveguessed unless you offered (or if you prefer proffered or more properly poppered) certain uncertain conjectives andor refutations...anyway being late for masswas definitely out of habbit (what had shebeen doing out of habbit I askew) and S.M.Himself knew that you could onlyblame the hand ofgod so far, there wasno excuse, excuse me she said as she pushedpast (but gently sister, gently, pax ta, and thankyou too went the Samoanpoet)...so she got to herseat she knelt downon the kneelers called herknees, nees being her maiden name, and she begat to pray mea culp mea culpa mea maximaculpa are you alright sister she heard a voice whisper which thought she had the hiccups and the Samoan looked shockedand off ended at hearingsome one men tion big things in church especially a woman of the cloth, maypy shehas other happits like rappits Paxta thought trying piously to laugh not...but Sister Mary H was preparing (prepa ringing somewhere in her bi psyche the litle green wheels were following, ono not I agin stabbing that picture with a Bowie knife where, will it end? Samsung he went to Perth waiting for his own birth through county Clare mea Clare mea Clare mea maxima Clare its a boy tits of milk to feed him Samuel is born and is borne around but the father petersout cant stay the distance of this dance of another wahine toa, taku tuahine, kia kaha, kia aroha haere kia taku manawa, hokia mai kia taku oranga - ka pai, tino pai tau tamaiti, taku iramutu - Samuel Becket is born!) for her confession...should she goto communion with such blackstain on hersoul, normallynot, but this was different! (there's avast deferens between menand women ma frenzy, but this time nun!) forit was the thirteenth dayafter death and she was nothingif she wasnot super stitious, thatis she believed! She dida quick act...of contrition and once again she knelt at the altar asa bride of Christ withher mouthopen, readyto receive Hisbody...Preasta, quaesumus omnipoteus. Deus (she was trans ported): ut anima famuli tui N. (famulae tuae Nnnnnn)...as the priest droned onshe started feeling agitated, her ordeal, a raw deal to be morep recise, was not longa way...how was shego ing to con fess cosi fan tutti that she had been dead for 13 days and that she wasa man to boot...the absolution took place on P1820 because the body wasntin church, but she, much to everyone's disgust (isafucken discustard, halloweenaloaya iseseen de MOONBOW!) shelet outa large giggleand a nervous fart, to some extent stifled by the gigglethough those closeto her knew it - she blew it...she knew the body was in church on the thirteenth, somewhat changed itis true, but there nun the less...collect (put in apocket)...Sand to rum at que electro rum, sodomy and the la ah ash...et rorum (largegirl, lookalike largiri) miser cordiae tuae peremnem infudas. Per Dominum...canyou keepa road secret that's myjob said Father...secret, munera...Quaesumus Domine quae tibi (quae tibi? what kind of talk is that! who let the rat in?) pro anima famuli, my family and other animals to you, tui N. (famulae tuae N. here's nottwo tuis in the trees), offerimus placatus (nothing can placate us!) intende: ut remedis pur-gata caelestibus (publica de transporta of heaven!) in tua pietate re-quiescat. Per Dominum (as usual)...soit came to postconununion tui rua o nga rakau...and where bound yes we are...Susipe Domine preces nostras pro anima famuli tui N. (formulae tuae N.): ut, si quae ei maculae de terrenis contagus, as she followed the words as they followed each other through the black mass book, missal if look at it, missile if you throw it, she felt the great surge of passion re kindle that she had for her wife (not her wife) when she had been a man...Seotho, a thoil, na goil go foill...he would sing to her, soas the priest was talking of contagiums she was think ingof hush darling...adheaserunt, remiss ionis tuae misericordia delantur. Per Dominum...Seotho a thoil! na goil go foill, Seotho, a linbh, a chumainn's a stor...S.M.H. was nearly crying somuch was the passion for his love but herehe was with a woman's body and living around the time of his future wife's (not his wife) birth, she looked out from the place of worship and saw a brandnew trolleybus (trolleybyceeee mygoan cornrade) making it's wayup collegehill, the roadstill looking patchy from where the tramlines had been lifted...Mo chuig ceod cumha go dubhach faoi bhron, Tu ag sileadh na sul is do chom gan lon! Nouse being hungry aswell as sad, mylove...so she re mem ers in the future onenight when they take time out tobe to gether (he was on the afterwards train where he vowed to get her, his strength surged through his body as he thought of the moment der zug entered mihiwaka and darkness) your hands are full of passion and they fold over mine like a baby's, she said Seotho a thoill, na goil go foill, Do gheobhair gan dearmad taisce gach seoid, nodont cry just yet my love my treasure (not his wife, not her wife) Do bhi ag do shinsear rioga ronihat (not Homburg nein) In - Eirinn iath-ghlais Choinn is Eoghaim (is what?)...five hundred sorrows, you are crying and I lament as the train goes, stops briefly at Purakanui and Waitati, and then works and winds its way round Parimoana, the cliffs and the sea wild and changeable as the great feelings of his pass (i) on...and as helooks out now he sees, at sundown, the talltrees on the horizon, the harbour headsand the delicate merging of colours ofindeterminate shapes,...has he lost her before he ever gother, the questions of all lovers dream through his being, can their love be of this world and as hemoves through te wahi moemea i rotoi te waka ia he feels the pain and the joy of life...theyholdhands and talk...she avoids his eyes and his embrace is awkward, avuncular, they not yet free...Ni gheallfad uaim duit duais nios mo...no more rewards can be promised so all hehears is the evening train heading towards Puketaraki past 339 and his melancholia is compleat...quam immolando totius mundi tribuisti relaxam delicta. Per Dominum...ut per haec piae placationis officia perpetuam misercordiam consequatur Per Dominum nostrum...so a woman's secret is different toa man's even unto death, she thought to himself, and she heard the priests last drones...et in nomine patri, et filu, et spiritus santus aman (amine) and she, Sistermaryhimself shehe would have to confess allher known and unknown sins: past and future in thought, word and deed (indeed), through myfault, throughmy fault, through my most grevious fault...being aman anda woman there was so many sins and temtations to reveal and reject, so many more evil thoughts and words and deeds to do and think about: how could shedo it and not leave somthingout...as she made her way from the church to the separate building where there's a guy whosegot religionhe'll tell youif your sin's original, she noticed that the brandnew trolleybus, which replaced Billythebus and Teddy (the toxin) tram had lost its poles off the wire at threelamps...as she looked out through the eyeofgod shesaw, seesaw, forty yearson...(13) orthere abouts, people bleeding to death in the morning ara by the sea moana and the restwerein mourning, ashelooked out from pari moana as dusk of the secondday of massacre descended the usual beauty of southern evening the evilsoul of people abstracted itself like a hidden andun seen surrealmontage ...centturies oldland scape against minutes old murder, just round the corner, littlejack, historical murderingbeach just round the reverse corner hysterical scenes of death, nonbreath, bereavement sadnessin responseto madness...another persongone porangi but it wasn't that easy, shit, T.V. image versus tranquil antiquity of the reality of the eyo god...evil sin evils in the heart of people this time expressed in semi-automatic style, bulletsbang and the coastghost is resurrected, everything looks good in black and white, greyimages, dullness of spirit, describedagain Sister, godeeper the eyogod is thefu turetobe, or not tobe the same as the past, present us Sister with the facts...a house is burnedout...the deathtoll mayrise, allsouls daymass...whatever happens the death toll will rise, he wishes she was here withhim, like your master's kingdom our lovecrypt perhaps, cannotbe of this world...but he loves her just the same, his passion permeates the daysemotion, looking out to the ocean, pacific, unlike the events of the northern headlands, the spit the spirit of ancient pre-verbal com...no com...no com... union (unholy) had the? so surely not but you neverknow do you...BANG, BANG you're dead, a bullet hereanda bullet there, here abullet, there abullet, everywherea bulletbullet...but that's not for forty years, she thought do I haveto confess that as theeye of god closes yet again on humanaffairs (all he wants is a humanaffair with her, that's one thing for sure, sharing warmth and love and humour they know is in both of their hearts but the risksare great) evenboats can't enter the harbour as sheenters the confessional shedoes the signof thecross and saysto herself "I cannot prevent what will happenin Aramoana, I cannot Save Aramoana from my vision of carnage but 1 will prayfor the living and the dead"...the trains stillrumble past, and is allaround but their sightis un seen, even the trees that normallyblock knowledge (visual a visual train) cantbe seen because of blackness, melancholia or otherwives that's the way itgoes, tusalava...only twentyfour hours from tusalava, onlyone dayaway from id dhoid, or thereabout...titiro ki te whetu whero, ai whetu whero-whakara i te rau o te patu...who said that...there is some thingin theair...meahiccup meahiccup meahiccuphiccup andeven asshe spoke this visionof terror in futuretimes distressed blessme fatherfor I havesin nedit is twodays today sincemy last con fess ion aeons itseems like light years agoand it seemslike yes terday but notto day and since then I have...silence descended like the blanket of nightfall on the unsuspectingland butit was uneasy, shit, and her mind was like a wallof graffiti just before itis discovered bya righteous up standing member...the stillness inside that little box was notcalm but menacing, threatening likea darkalleyway whereyou can still seeshadows and flickers of lightand life...kaore mataku au, shethought kia kaha au!, and with this she said, while the priest listened, relieved that sound of windandlimb signifying something had again entered the worldof light...I have never fucking sinned in my fucking life, shebe gan slowlyand deliber atelymutedelatedly...notin action (killed inaction means action) no I have never doneone fuckingthing that couldbe interpreted (letsnot pretend) as being bad, but...at this the priesthe recovered from his reeling shocksand prepared for after shocks which he knew wouldbe morede vastating because now that the found ations have been shaken itwas only left for the edifaces and erections to fall...nungoeson mangoes in syryp eatall, sickly...ina jar allways keep a jar of new jam on the windowsill leaving the window ajar har har har ha har...the sewer of nunsmind is seeping somany some, any years of blocked emotion, effluent pours fluently out through pores of souls and other holes such as assholes, one word she has saidbe forein secret, secretion of shit sap and nuncum...1 have had somany sodomy (like a romany my mother said I nevershould) times forlornly forn icated in my mindseye and otherplaces 1 have eaten dogs shit and pulled mybra (not unlike a sticky hydra) and pants down, a clown in front of young children and bade them come and touch me asof I them, touch me badly like an evil forbidden fruit...I turned on and got turned onby, the gas ovens of Triblinka, I didn't even blink as I wat ched all them people dying by myhand you under stand that when I was a child on myfirst holy communion I vowed to Jesus never to sin and in doingso 1 have neverstopped sinning since...know ledge, the ledge of knowing over whichis going my thoughtsof goodand evil, shooting rapids of words and deeds liftup your dress, takedown your tweeds: shakedown...fucka duck comecuntcum quid pro quo away wego with a great big negro mutherfucker (yes that too) incest a game the whole family can play gameatazoa tis as gayas theycome ACDC ETC but the worst ofall is I know when to stop...I have pure shit thoughts pureshit father pureshit but live a life of purityand chast titty who wants a titty tit swill de, tit willdo and a dildo, but why wherefor art the bigcock and the tightlittlecunt of desire how can I goon thinking thus and living thither, help me shithead for I have tinned thyballs and willyeat them for gaters with potaters and shesobbed out of relief and grief, shehad wanted to tell himof her really being a man, not a transvesper exactly but a real man except with awo mans body bodidly bodily and there was somuch left unsaid and uncovered...the priest, whowas really the skull of Samuel Becket inside whicha light shone at regular intervals, an affectation of acting tobe sure or not I says he and which had being travelling through the suburbs eightfoot tall on the back ofa trailer leaning the righthemisphere and nowlies splitin two Onehunga (there are many hungry but only One) keeping the wood from the door, slowly says to her, sister 1 feel your anguish, 1 feel your pain...absolution, and your penance is three hail marys and one how's your father...come in peace, go in pieces I'll see you round the back in fifteen minutes...like two colourless orshould I say blackandwhite angels they flewtogether on their wings of desire and landing neara town called Munchen they thought they metall the people they knew, all the people of this Germancity were people they, of course, didntknow but theyall had faces and bodies and clothes of the two angels dearest friends but they didnt know them sothey sattogether in the cafe taking timeout to begin toget to know each other like twopeople whohad just met holding handsand talking forhours andhours then they flewoffsky ward over Poland and sepa rated agreeingto meetin the dream in Los Angeles or New York whence heandshe would dream in Ireland but the heangel was lastseen heading towards the city of the angels (lost) faithless and unfaithful giving in to temporal temptations as the express thundered through the night of the nineteen fourties. I've got to meether, I've got to meether clickety clack clickety clack I've got to meether and clickety clack so the angels were human afterall, should have stayed for lunchin Munchen munch munch...butnow the nun Sistermaryhimself was preparing toleave, even though she hadnt told all, shestill had sinon her soul she still had dreams andmad ness (the locked up monster) she wouldwander to the end of her time with the spectre of darkness in her heart but as sheheard the priest's footfalls coming across to give herher penance she couldnot stand the thought of himbeing on topof and inside her hisgrunting and snorting of sexualstabs madeher feelrepulsive for whileshe knew the virginbirth was an almighty cockup shehad little hope for the Lord's earth minions, mini ons, soshe ranfor it rather than stay waiting forit...when she was young kidsused totalk of digging ahole to China through the earth so S. M. Himself pickedupa spade and with the thought "I'lldiga hole to Ireland," she set to work...when she haddug enough (two miles as the wormflies) a greathunger setin, soshe rested anyway and hermind went straight out of it justas the priest Father O'Blivion had disappeared through the blackhole of hermind asshe had hoped and not through the blackhole of herbody as he hadhoped, nunshe thought howshe blasphemed and that more through crowded confused streets, jumpeda board anold photograph (or wherethey alwaysyou) pera i te marama kahuna kou i another porangi kaere au i mohio ana otira rete he tamaititangohia ia tahi hikoi precious andhid den while studying at Trinity hewas usinghis position as she used violent stabswithher fingers asthe childis afraid of falling this karanga of the poly nesian woman before he drewhis handand made aswipe and letfly, mercy ofgod the sunhad just burstthrough and was in the eyes or he'd beenleft fordead, God hewas nearly sentinto the confetti graveyard about the earlike (better buyan earwig to keep the hearingwarm) a message to the hearingvolk, listen! forall the populace shouting another, a not her round as the laughing forseen poteen event was stopped from having him P.S.M. dragged along like anold tinbox chattering along the street, kept mefromgo inginsane, life wenton like that again through a field onher (offer) way the grasswas wet and over leaned the path she heldher skirts sensationally up andnot because thegrass waswet and sweet and sweat o'the brow because aman, P.S.M. was watching she wasin love with passion and its weakness that wetgrass couldnot cool radiated from her unwanted womb in that country, in that metaphysical land (twomiles down) where fieshwas a thought more spiritual (unlike carnal victual) than music. Among the stars out of reachof the peasant hand...kei te mokemoke au under mountains you carry the weight of my passions she said if you want to callme ina hurry dial nein, nein, nein, in otherwords dont callme! Ich bin von Munchen munch munch, is deacair teacht yes I knowbut, about it he is impotent ni feidir leis teacht, d'iarras air teacht: perhaps someone will teach him. Butaft era few daze of diggin it S.M. Him selfish asit was (not shellfish) decided she didnt digit nomore, sowith only as light error of Judgement Day she turned around having goneonly twentyfive (25) miles towards Ireland through the centre of the earth and she came out of the ground near Punakaiki, butthen looked enough for life tobe the Giant's causeway of Ant cluchaun na Vomore ach anyway so giant pancakes it is all round and there's Rita taking her first steps, practicing for alps, out of loneliness and homesickedness, start somewhere you know, youknow. Rita points the bone towards the place of Sister Joyce orat least Joyce's sister who when they meet throws upher armies in exasperation "an leabhar san Sheamais" and then again, "an obair seo na

Gaelige" but then doesn't she give the nunsister Maryhimself a big welcome to the Westcoast and listens to her story laughing and after the feast of the Iclassl kyrie fans bonitatis kyrie eleison (before kiritekanawa, daughter of . . .) gloria in excelsis Deo, daughterof...Et in terra pax he - minibus to Hokitika, usedtobea railcar from Ross bonae vo-lunta tis laudamus te. Bene Hill dickimus te. Adoramus te. Glorificamus te, now finish up your tea and we will goto bed...Sisterjoice and sisterhimself layin eachother's arms afterorgasm both feeling replete, the great togetherness of two people cometogether in love, drifting off to sleep together and separately, whispering the odd involuntary word one to the other meaningless in context but full of the wonder of nomeaning love and ancient knowledge that no wakingday world can understand as their breasts touch each others lightlynow, Gratias agimus tibi propter magnana glorian tuam. Cum Sancto Spiritu in gloria Dei Patris, A-men . . .

3

One dream S.M.H. had as shelay with Sister Joyce that eve ning took her entirely away sothat when Joyce's Sister awoke in the morning expectingto find her lover she was no longer there andshe neversaw her again...Himself somewhat taken abackin time and place butnow restored to manhood wherewas he now, didhe workupon the railway, didhe ridthe streets of grime, without the headof, must be headingoff now, the great white mass ofan anglican party wasin half-swing, protesting ants, cat a holicks spilling drinkon the fair dinkum richwhite car pet, poodlestrudel, nolight flickering onoroff, nobright ideas only the steady dullduty bound lives of the flock, no flocknocker except for sleeping, no tortured souls no laughing no weeping, godhelps those that help themselves so helpyourselves and to hell with the rest, no rest for the wicked, I'm so tired, I havent slept awink a ship of light sailsby in the darkness, metaphor omo metaphor it's realenough and Himself has taken ona seriarse ness which belies his out wardgoingnature, where is henow, heknows but wont let thecat out of thebag despite the inter minableisland ferrymeowing shutup, boot! He dreams he wasa nun, flying zip undone, he dreams he wasa snow man lying bleeding on loves stoneywhite ground, but now the dreamis over, what can say, the bubblesburst of love again no romantic beauty inner orouter, just stones and facts, survival tactics not evena did you know? ora howa bout this! Workether, ethics of dollarbill birds, queensface smearedsmirkinglike filth, the smir king major itty, no titty, not the Filthy Few factsand figures Irish population (due entirely to copulation in the firsinst) of Otago shotup, Shotover 3,154 (eleven p.c) from 206, 1861, and then in Cromwell, nay Lowbum, O'Brien wasshooting at those who went buy elswhere, I'll take you homea gain Kathleen, no youwont be causeshe's dead, but has risena gain oursister welcome as prophesised in the holy youknowwhat, where did you get that what, but the houris getting late and the child, I mean trial is a bout to begin beit gin orbit of whiskey be gin the child, 1 mean trial of Archbishop Liston for treason trees are green, Teresa after the Easter Proclamation came one of many childs from everywhere, I mean trials from out of the Roisin Dub, from the dark just after the Shoneen, butfrom inside the Rosaleen, herself as to opposed to himself united but still fighting in Himself, from between the sheets on the occasion...Twopenny O'Reagan and Conlan himself defended at the child of Bishop Liston, not yetarched and I mean trial, S means all my trials, Lord, soon be october, the month of Our Lady...Patrick Fitzgerald stepped down off the planeat Mangere Air Port tired and still...and ??, thus calledbe cause when asked by hispoorer clients howmuch he wouldcharge to defend them would invariably reply "Oh, notmuchmore than twopence I cant imagine," started his intro into his defencecouncil summing up withnot the customary "May itplease yourhonour, Mr Foreman and gentle menof the jury etc," but with the more unauthordox, seditious even, phrase "What the fook is Patrick Fitzgerald doing here, stepping down off a plane which hasn't been invented at an airport which hasn't even been fooking builtyet!" "Order! Order!" cried the Stringing judge and immediately awaiter appeared witha pencil and notepad. However, Mr Conlan whispered something into Mr O'Reagan's ear, who then muttered "Mmmnmmmn, 1 see," and the judge seeing that things were atiast inorder, dismissed the waiter and said, "You may proceed Mr O'Reagan."...trying toget usedtohis newname. My name is James O'Donnell, he kept repeating to himself (is it himself?) in his own mind...the section of the Crimes Act under which the Bishop is indicted is declatory of the common law. The Crown Prosecutor has already indicated that here-lieson the twosub sections, U2, withor without you too section 118...Also in his own mind he keptre peating the image of the young Britishsoldier he had killednot aweek before, It had takenone thousandy ears of English oppression, allthe storiesfrom the oldones...which made it seditious touse words...told with the terrorof brutal reality being relived of the Blackand Tandays, all the horror of the re cent troubles since 1969...calculated to raisedis content or dis affection among Newzealand citizens, orto pro mote illwill and hostil itybe tween...all the memories of the maimed and murdered friends and family dealt to by these Brittish guardians of liberty it had taken all these things Russian through hismind like a streamofsky suddenly swollen anddang erous from flooding emotion...different classes of citizen. The real question is what did the Bishop intend? Of course, toa large ex tent, his intention is tobe gathered from the lanuage he used (English, sohis intention was obviously questionable) but...toget Patrick Fitzgerald to pull the triggeron this young english soldierboy. Notlong (the palandrome for notlob would be bolton) before, this soldier had been an arrogant, self-assured memb er of the best trained street armyin the world, meteringout British Justice to the savage, uncivilised Irish...in its verynature the definition of sedition is vague. Thus it becomes afact, a question offact, and hence one solefor the jury, after herring counsel's addresses (and telephone numbers as the Bishop said to the actress) and sub jectto the ass istance of Honour's review of the law and evidence...Now he was more like a squealing pig (is a pigsarse still porkdoctor dean?) writhing and pleading for mercy. Then there was nomore arguing. "You showed my people no mercy," Fitzgerald said quietly and pulled the trigger...Of course when the language is so plain that it speaks for itself the duty of the jury is mucheasier and shoulda persona directly incite others to violence or crime of anykind they will notbe allowed toplead the innocence of their motive or the goodness of their object, or to vary the plain meaning of their language..."Mr James O'Donnell," the customs officer looked at him, wanting a response. Pat rick lookedat the uniform and fora ninstance had for gotten his newidentity. Hewas justa bout tosay Fitzgerald whichwas hisown name which hisown mother hadgiven him at childbirth...Here ofcourse the case isnotso serious, butit will doubt lessbea greed that the language employed, asex plained in the evidence evidently is very differ entfromthat which appear edin the Pressre ports of the Bish opspeach..."Oh, yes, I'm sorry. Sure I'm james O'Donnell bit tired youknow itsa longa longalong flight from London and yougetta fewof the drinks downyou on the way, ha!"...you will agree with me having regard to the highoff ice of the Bishop, his frankness (no letmebe Frank, youwere him last night!) in the witness-box, and his satisfactory (isn't that the place where thy make satis, now Michael) mannerin which heex plained the meaning of his speech..."Have you anything to declare, Mr O'Donnell?" "Only megenious in the traditionof meancestors!" The official offal blackbottle waved himon in amanner which said typical bloodymad Irish, "Next!" Sweet Saint Patrick, thatwas close, Patrickmuttered to himself (again what was himself doing there when he should have been attending to the child, I mean trial of Bishop - of the 1920s - Liston this man himself was beginning to take on certain characteristics ofthe man Himself, frightening in its enormity!) as he made his wayout of the customs area to collect hisbags and lookfor the person hewas tomeet...not merely that hehadno malicious in tent, or anyother unfixed abode, but that hehad been the victim of much unnecesssary and coarse criticism and that the indictment canin no way be sustained (in Norway?) In connection with the speech Gentlemen, it isnot anti cipatedthat youwill necessarily agree with all the views therein expressed...ashe lookeda round the concourse (brothers) the first thing that struck himwas the numberof darkskinned people. It wasa real surprise for him (a real surprise for himyummmmnunm!) for the onlything he really knew a bout N.Z. was that it wasa country which strove tobe more English than the English...everyone is entitled to their opinions on the questionof the day and in this respectone citizen isas good asanother. Moveover, what doyou mean I mean moreover, they are entitledto persuade othersto share their views on as I shallshow presently shellshock, thereis nolimit in this respect save that theymay notemploy improper language, norad vocate violins to attain their end, if there's music in hell it will beplayedon bagpipes, Jimmy said that...the iron icnature of this amused him and he was laughing to himself (whoelse?) about how the peoplehe camefrom were known as the Black Irish not to mention the Puck himself (also) when his thoughts were interrupted byaman saying "Hey bro, are you James O'Donnell?"...now, having heard the evidence after the eveningdance I askew to dismiss from your minds asfaras possible the aspersions castupon the Bishopby the Press andby various public bodies and to judge him onlyon what you have heard in this court. Not only have the witnesses for the Crown been serverely shaken in cross-examination but severalof them have admitted that the Bis hop, when dealing (hop) with the Easter uprising and subsequent events, stated that hewas reading from alist andeven they weresat isfied that when his Lordship spoke about the 155 men and women, three of whom were priests (but we'll neverknow which, nun but Himself knows) who during and since 1916 had diedfor Ireland, hewas not referring only to those who who were killed in the Rising, but also those who who were conceived and born because of the "rising"...unsettled and stunned he answered "Yes." As he collected himself (where did he collect himself from?) and hisluggage together he looked at the tall, well-built Maori man whohad greeted him. His thoughts were wild but he said, "How doyou knowmyname? I was supposed to meet some one called Paddy O'Connell." "Yeah, that's me," the man smiled and gave Fitzgerald an unfamiliar street-wise handshake. They both walked silently towards the bar andit was only when they both hada pint of beer before them that O'Donnell felt relax edenough to speak to O'Connell...and thathe referred to the Black and Tansalone, not justas a mixture of beerandstout, but as also murderers foremost. Even asit stands the speech unex plained by evidence cannotbe reason ablysaid tobea damaging inferences which the Crown (the Brattish Croam, as van the man might say) seeks to draw therefrom. Taking the first para graph onwhich witch the Crown relies hislord ship, any thing goes in, anything goes out the snake winds around bothhere and about, early in the speech referred the numbers of Irish people whohad beendriven from their homes because their foreign masters didnot want the landpeopled by Irish menandwomen but preferredto makeit a cattlerach for the snobsof the empire, the Irish umpire raised his finger in the air indicating notout..."Andyou know aboutme then now, do you Paddy?" Fitzgerald asked halfchallenging hishost and halfhoping that hewas surelya mong friends. "Oh, yeah," answered Paddydrinking, Paddy, Drink King, his beer with a great relish, not in a pickle, "But I think the least said the bet tera round here, e?" By the time they left the air port, brandy, whiskey, gin (thatswhat did me in) both men had drunkand talked enough to be completly re laxed in each other's company. They strode out towards the car park, where the cars play calling Mr Carswell, tap this well and we're away, singing and shouting at the tops of their voices twentyfourhours from Tulsa they were happy...here the Bishop wasal luding to an historical fact, an his tooori caal fa aaaaa act, a deplorable fact, a de plooour ableee faa aa a ct, you will remembergentlemen, that hewas speaking to an Irish audience on a subject which the Irish heart beat feels deeply. It maybe diffi cult foryou who are not Irish to under stand that feeling. But as the Lybian writer of yore, and yours!, Sheik el a Bar, says "He jests at scars, that never felt a wound"...Paddy's car wasan oldbeat up Mark II Zephyr, west wind haiku

Zephyr west wind, to you

A poem was written

This is mine Mark 2

and Patrick noticed how differentit looked to the other cars belonging to the moreaffluent air portpatrons, the BMWs, Mercedes, and myriads of latemodel Japanese cars. "They'll never suspectus in this Paddy, they think the IRA are all millionaires from Lybia." O'Connelllauugh andswung the carinto the mainroad towards the motorway...I trust, however, you possess sufficient of the dramatic instinct toput yours elves in our place, O'Reagan continued (whilst smiling ironically to himself, who in turn smiled back as if to say thatsa bit below the belt 2d, accusing the English of dramaticin stinct) for I am proud to be of Irish ex tractionmy self, and not to make false a, near the beach of Tusitala llowance for

Llewellyn whenhe comes running but to feel some sympathy for the sentiment of deep indig nation...Patrick was struck by two (more later) main things as the car roared along towards Auckland City. The first was the light, the quality of brilliance and sharpness in the sky and secondly he hadn't expect ted Auckland tobe sobig and modern. The crack was good be tween the two as the car rattled and hummed a long the motorway. Patrick said to Paddy "Have many of the Maoris got the Irish names like your self now?" "Ah, yeah bro! We got alot in common, e! Here," he said handing Fitzgeraldd a bottle of beer, "I'd rather have a bottleinfrontofme than a frontalabottomy he he he, ai! But apart from the fact that my greatgreatgreat grandfather hada bit ofa liking for the duskymaidens whohid him when he wason the run for deserting during the landwars, there is quite a lot of overlaps between our two cultures"...with which they'd recall the evictions which drove such immense numbersof Irishpeople from their country and which accounts in no smallmeasure for the abiding affection rnanyof their descendants still cherish, is the word association footfall softly, softly, for the landofsky their ancestors who suffered such cruel and in excusable wrongs...Patrick drank and listened as Paddy parallelled the two races, Galway and Wingatui, their love of fighting and their love of art, their strong oral tradition and love of words, their poetic legends and mythologies...mylearned friend invites you to take seriously the paragraph in which the Bishop states that Erin has not got all she asked for, not all that her sons and daughters died for, but that she had secured an in stalment of her free domand was determined to have the whole, til death duty parts...here Patrick began to laugh. "What's funny?" asked Paddy...the vast majority of Irish people share the feeling and it is absurd to suggest that the views expressed by Bishop Liston are anything other than that which any citizen is entitled (and indeed should O'Reagan thought to himself, who concurred)..."I've gota friend in Dublin who fancies himself a bit of a poet," said Fitzgerald, "Brendan that's his name, now he wrote a poem once about a friend of ours called the Ballad of Ryan O'Corky." "Lets hear it, bro," said Paddy and Patrickre cites thus
His skin was bumpy, palid and chalky
Yet this never held him back
For he was ethnic without being black

at this theyboth cracked-up laughing...the commendation of Mr de Valera as the manwho has carried Ire land thus far and who wouldsee that the leadersof Irelandwere not duped by England is also wellwithin the boundsof freespeech, a freebee for a bone..."Ha, thats real funny about being ethnic without being black. I remember readinga book when 1 was last inside by Robert Graves, e, where he said one of the things which blew the Englishaway when they camehere was the similarity be tween the Maori tribal setupand the old Irish wayof doing things the tohanga, the whole bit. That probably made them even more determined to undermine Maoritanga, ai"...though the passage would certainly have been less liable to mis interpretation, more especially as thereis criticism this country iseagerto mis interpret, had the Bi shop make itplain that he ref erred to the Government and not the peopleof en gland...travelling along Tamaki Drive towards Orakei bothmen wentsilent enjoying the beauty of the trees, thesky, the water. The car turned into Watene Crescent. "Come on bro, haere mai, welcome to home."...His Irish audience under stood what he meant, indeed they have too many historical reasons for doingso...Patrick looked at the statehouse where he would beliving andas hewas surrounedbya sea of brown smilingfaces asall the childrenin the neighbour hood collectedex citedly hewas thinkingof hisown home asmall councilhouseinthe south of Ireland...I referto that of the pressreport which has givenrise to the stron gestde nun ciation. I concede atonce that the in dictment would befully just ified if the Bishop reallyspoke as the pressreports him. Assuredly, how ever, he has abundantly satisfied you...James had been introducedto the family. Also, the Auckland Sinn Fein man came tosee him to give him money and tell him a bout the lie of the land. "You'll be layin' low fora bit, and then wewant a few things done." "What's that now Danny?"...that he did not apply the word "murdered" in connection with those who were killed inaction in 1916, and that he only used the term in connection with the Blackandtans during 1921..."Well, Patrick we know there are U.D.R. men herin New Zealand wholike yourself are on the run and have been given new identities. Unlike yourself these boysare here with the complicity of the British Government and possibly the New Zealand Government is involved inan even more active way than just turning ablindeye"...here let me state that we cannot recede from our contention that the men and women of the blackandtans were murderers..."So it was formore than just the humanitarians that you got me out here." Daniel O'Brien looked at this young killer and all the feelings for the land he wasof but had never been to came upon him. For a moment Patrick became O'Brien's own ancestor standing before him, his grand father driven into escape and exile for being a murderous Fenian bastard, an Irish savage, for fighting to regain his country from the English rulers...the plain people of Ireland, indeed the people of the Irish race everywhere, hold in reverence the menandwomen whohave foughtand bled for the cause of nationality...O'Brien said "the Maori people in New Zealand notonly have a similar outlook and culture to our own but their struggle to be who they are in their own country is also the same, and it is basically against the same system and people...just as they revere Robert Emmet, who engaged in a forlorn hope, they cherish the memories of those who died in 1916"...Is there any IRA type Movement that the Maori people fight under? In the past there were many rebel groups who opposed British rule and the Treaty of Waitangi but they got heavily stamped on especially when the settlers arrived to claim "their land" which had been promised to them...may I remind you finally, thatone of the men involved in the Easter Rising was Michael Collins whowas sub sequently Commander-in-Chief of the Irish Republican Army but who is now a minister of the crown aman who the peopleof both countries feeland hope will domuch to reconcile the two nations...your jobis to breakinto the UDR exile scheme and expose it, we've actually got a lead onone of them who lives herein the Eastern Suburbsof Auckland who we think you willbeable to identify...bear in mind thatin everyage and everycountry history records acts of heroism which were illegal and atleast as faras the chiefact ors were concerned, futile and disastrous...Patrick Fitzgerald fell asleep almost immediately anditwas the firstime ina week that whenhe closed hiseyes he didnot see the eyesof his victim looking at him in terror...I am convinced, having regardto hishigh office, the fact that hisco-religionists are a small minority in this country and the frank (and earnest) and ready mannerin which he has demeaned him selfin the wit nessbox, that you willagree the Bishop and the actress cannot lightly be presumed to have intended sedition...cruising along Kepa Rd., the reggaebeat pounding them towards the Glen Innes pub. Wakeup tomorrow with the G.I. blues e, bro, said Rewi. I reckon Rangireplied and theyall laughed...remember that within the limits I havequoted everycitizen is legallyfree to express whatever opinion they please...as soonas they walked through the door O'Donnell gota fix on him. He hadnt seenhim forfive years but Patrick would haveknown him blindfolded as indeed hehad when William Craig, Sergeant in the UDR had taken him in for questioning about anarms ship ment meant for the IRA theyhad held him for forty hours with a hoodover his head and no food...but these are politicalquestions andyou donot need telling that politicalquestions areoft sandwitched with the fiercest passion...he had raised Craig's ire bymerely suggesting that itwas the UDR whowere the real terrorists in Ireland the fact that theygot their weapons supplied freeby the English didn't make them more moral, only legal under Brittish law...those who profess unpopular opinions or principles not properly under stood areoft exposed to unfair attack by opponents whomakea cheap parade of loyalty to the established orderof thingsby levelling lying accusations of dis loyalty or dat loyalty hey sorry you aint the child of Bishop Liston is you, you mean trial, man, oh yeah! and sedition against brave and upright citizens...he went and called Paddy and told him what wasup I wasn't expecting this despite O'Brien's briefing, anyway you'd better get overhere, overthere, overhere, and Paddy, come prepared. He went back to the bar and told the others he was just going to get a bit of freshair, he didnt want to lose Craig..."Wehaveno King but Caesar" shouted the Scribes and Pharisees of Jerusalem longago was sofar togo, sofaa soifua, and againsaid theyto Pilate, punch us, "If thou release Himself thou art not Caesar's friend." Yet they hated

Caesar andall that his Governmentmeant. They affected loyalty to Caesar because they desired to have Himself declared guilty whom they accused of stirring up sedition...suddenly he was grabbed around the throat and he felt a pistol stuck into his back. "So its james O'Donnell is it, aye!" The Irish werealways a bloody literary lot of lunatics, right Jimmy. But we know who you murdering Papists are killing young Brittish soldiers nowarewe, ha!" Craig held thegun to Fitzgerald's head...itis not without reason that a distinguised historian has said thatno legal process hasbeen more shamelessly perverted to tyranical andun just ends than that of treason and sedition...Craig cocked the pistol and with his finger on the trigger, said "the world wont miss the death of another" and a shot rangout. Patrick looked around in wonder that hewas still alive. He thought he had been shot but Paddy grabbed himby the arm, "Lets get out of here, bro! Here catch!" Fitzgerald caught the rifle as they both got in the Mark 11 and spedoff into the night...Dr Liston really said nothing which he orany other citizen hadnot a perfect right to say, but by publishing a garbled condensation ofhis speech, servedup under misleading headlines and criticising its own version the press inflamed the publicmind to an extent that would have been impossible were it not for the fact that the speaker was a Catholic Bishop...the next morninga report appeared in the paper headed GANG KILLING, Aman by the name Sammy Cordon believed tobea member of a white rights gang, was shot dead outside the Glen Innes Tavern last night. Police said two men, believed to be Maori or Polynesian were seen leaving the hotel in a Zephyr car which was later found in Tautari St, Orakei, Police also said they were looking fora .22 rifle no other weapon was involved...having heard the Bishop's evidence and his trans parent (you see I told you there was a child and that the Bishop was a parent doesn't matter howit happened trans or other wise virgins its always been apparent) confidence toyou tofind a verdict truthfulness and accordingly I appeal with Not Guilty...which was the judge meant and so it was and as Conlan and O'Reagan went off to gether in opposite directions him self stood looking, watching and waiting for his wife not hiswife andas they embraced his head was full of skull...a great sadness swept overhim, overtime, all down the days he realised no matter howmany lives he lead how many incarnations how many carnal dreams or spiritual thoughtshow old they lived to be, how close they came to...their love could not be of this world and he wept silent and inwardly for he knew that even if he lived to be a thousand year reich ora million dollar rich that he had met the woman he loved, which is more than a lot of people do, but that they could never be of this world...a great storm blew up and the sky darkened and her image also darkened but he knew she would always return with each flash of lightning, with each roll of thunder and then the rains would beat heavily completely engulfing the headland and he never felt more alone...c1920 the head or rather the skull of becket would not of been as well formed and it would come to be so that when himself first discovered it it was more likely full of crecket or silent movies and after the trial of the child of Mrs Liston had been witnessed he picked up the empty skull holding it out stretched in one hand proclaiming alas poor sam we will know him well but at this stage we are still waiting for not I butyou...are a simpleton...But he loved the flight of the hawk and could distinguish it from all others. He would stand rapt, gazing at the long preenings, the quivering poise, the wings lifted for the plummet drop the wild reascend, fascinated by such extremes of need, of pride, of patience and solitude himself turned almost automatically from his wifeless reveries into a hawk and with quick glance overhis shoulder at what mighthave been he flew soaring southwards in the past...

4

Angry and frust rated the hawk flapped its wings violently inside its cage making a loud, piercing sound...its owner wasdrunk again and the hawk hated this neglect, it called and called again but the man was hunched overa writing desk and every nowand again would turn around and yell fuck up and throw anyhandy object at the bird, so that all around the cage were littered an odd assort mentof shoes, slippers, pens, pecnils an inkwell etc the man re turned to his activities which were pre ceded by a rather large swigfroma bottleof whiskey. He then pickedup oneof the few rem aining pens onhis desk and began rewritting...the hawk, himself looked maliciously towards the paper on which Paddy Murphy was scribbling and crossing out and re doing lines as he gargled and gurgled whiskey intermittently between words, hawkeye read, redeye hawked, te himene o Aotearoa at the topof the page scrawled on halfwaydown Guard Pacifics tripled star, from the shaft of mines, and yours, this last piece had a line through it and the exasperated author finallysick of trying to writea rose and taking a final swig of the water of life anda swingat the cage of the nowresting bird lurched outinto the street of his Elders, he wasa child of clones they're all the same these madirish...while Murphy presented himself at the barof the Waiting Arms to the soundof Irishrebelsongs and cry of have a Guiness Paddy calling from the future, the hawkhimself waslooking at the dateon the calendar, he couldonly makeout the year 1878 and the hawksquawked shrilly like rogers eaglehawk at the ignorance of the notknowing wing or prayer to flyon butonly cagedangst of existential forecasts...himselfhawk soon changed histune though, asthrough animaginary holein the door a tentative birdfoot is seen, thus fulfilling the scripture by their feets shall yeknow them...its rifleman titipounamu the firstshall belast zee zee goes darkbrownbill call made even morefeeble bya twigheld...hawkhim self courteousbut cold, says ka pai titi, e hoa, doesnt like consorting with smaller birds too much...hawkfeels morelike eating them but callsout for more pork from the Englishpig just to con fuse the issue forth or maybe fifth but he also pre pares fora succession of small birds who be gin and tonic the message procession in andout the imaginary door at the footof the realdoor...himself awaits herself at the tail end, dovetail to smoke precisely, but until te manu o aroha can come, other birds must arrive and leave leaving leaves, twigs, pieces of paper, wrigglyworms, string, and other things allof which will bewitch and be wilder with wilder or less tales from the wilderness and strangeness of Irishhistory in newzealand from the presentpast and future, 1878 the present hethinks to him self with hawkbrains ashe look with hawkeye at titi going zeezee zeezee zeeyou later kahu, e hoa, haere atu titi, ka pai e karere, ka pai nga kupu...himself hawk looks at the rifieman's twig and twigs to the message "Law proposed in Parliament to ban Irish settlers from coming to New Zealand" himself thinks mmmmm, and puts informationtwig ina pile marked present which he isa bout to begin, past and future piles will also be built as information comes to claw...haere mai, miromiro, comensie, comensie, in flits a yellow breasted tit, with a Japanese influence, axis bold aslove, Italia, quarrellsome as Ill Duce and justas lively, anold crinkled piece of paper, I have in myhand a piece of paper and he doesnt leave it but readsit "Jimmy Hendrix will play fora football gridiron team called The Fighting Irish and arguably willbe of Maori blood, nga puhi," he, or is it she, difficult to tell witha tit, garullously puts the paper in the futures, not shares, basked and leaves without somuch as a haere ra...himself, ina sort of people haze tries hard to think who, Jimmy who? He recalls from the past and the future and tries to think Jimmy who but in 1878 the words "Outside in the distance the windcries as the manwho is aslost asa child throws his round redball towards my bat which I hold erect, yeah man, the wind cries because this bloodred ball pierces the skin of the air, the wind cries with the awarenessofits own existence but the ball keeps coming and coming until it hitsmy bat and I'm running and the wind is crying"...just dont make sense and the hawk shakes the unhooded head of himself, thinking in wonderment that this is nojust out of it but out of out of it and then what does that mean in 1878, not..."spudmiss ile attack spud miss ile attack spud" - hey hey hawksay slowdown but upokotea whitehead goes on frantically "fired from van morris on the ramp and from all Ireland sites, covered with mashed potatoe to hide its whereabouts" give me that says himself and he grabs the piece of manuka - get your white head outa here hetells the confused little bird - and the hawkreads "The IRA today caused complete chaos in the centre of London by clogging the city with tons of potatoes fired from vans covered with false tops made from papier mache. Delivered by SPUD missiles each potatoe head was rumoured to be ableto carry chemical pesticides ona prepared speech a spokesman said that the attack was in retaliation from the potatoe famine and that if the crop didn't fail, there would be 'more where that came from.' Already major London Rail Stations have hadto be closed because potatoes have had trains losing their traction as potatoes, mixed with the snow and sludge turned lines into virtual"... but the hawkmust stop his reading about utu riwai as a commotion (loco) is going on outside hisdoor and he sees dozens of birds of all species trying desperately to getin through the imaginary doorway, theyall have bits of in formation which is gradually being broken or twisted or twittered outof control, in the din hawk getsfed by eye or ear morsels of framents from such as...a shybird, once bitten now matuku-hurepo singssong of potatoe family take me back to dear old blighty butso softly, softly, no one hears her there'll always behan England, til Ireland gets the bomb, get it...and Godwit is spreading a truemour about O'Ryan and Maher's and other pubs of the universe, Kuaka, morelike a halfwit...and he's coming in around thebend in the one mile handicap, does a black-fronted tern within twohundred yardsof the winning post the race seemed to belong, him bilong, blong, Edward Fitzgerald. The com petitorswere being keptcool by havingwater putover them, but instead of watersome person threw brandyin Fitzgerald's face and helost the race - whata place and that was the forerunner ofa marathon of the second lake, himself's ancestor, tipuna fitzgeraldo against herself's father dragging boats through the jungle butat different timesofcourse and mal adjusted to losing at chess to his son outlaw - e hombre thus sang the tara notfara way from Otara but asfor Tara or O'Zara that could besome way off in time and distance...wheredid you ever hear this, a little bird toldme so listen its tauraki from Invercargill yellowcrested and all a number of bailiffs were employed in each case, to suit, they read a war rant which went unheeded, the inmates werethen turnedout followedby theirscant belongings. The evictions were carriedout under the in structions of the Otago and Southland Investment companiesmother of all evictions and also of Mrs Cassidy, aged 80years, who hasspent allher life in the colonies, andover ???? nearly 30 years in the district, was dancinga round the policeman and bailiffs

yellingout "Thank God I have lived to seea real Irish Eviction." The evictions are dueto failureto pay rentto, July 17, 1889, oddity, froma penguin of the southernmostcoast...coldas toast, three chairs sitray, sitray sitray, birds andbits of formation flyinga round the room, Toms and tits, and 17th March St Patricia got down from her mount Ryan, and headed for Blackball, not my father's girlfriend surely thought himself, but no its time to re joyce again sister big conception not of possum borne but carried beyond and to re dress St Patrick, (of the different habbit) himself, St Patricia herself, now St Patricia herself, so the other side of the world, mirrors the other side of the world, a boy becomes a girl a merry virgin whirls embroidered hair twirls into curls, no churls, a woman's right to choose aspeaker dancing in Charleston demands in 1868 one hundred years be fore personal tragedy, Hey Jude, dont make it bad, "Do I, or any other Irishman owe allegiance to the British Crown" in Hokitika, Margaret rose and the response was "loud criesof No!" but 7 Fenians were secretly de tained oncharges of sedition and the colonywas safefrom the Connolly...Kariorio, a stoutgrey warbler is onabout semi-bestial savagery of Irish, distancing themself from the difficulty of calling for landrights in Ireland while imprisoning 200 Maori people, notrial, for insisting on their own landrights (c. or holysee 1879) and then, nga puhi, Hone Mohi Tawhai told a landleague meetingin Wellington in 1881 "the Irish cause is the cause of all men" andas the Irish soldiers fightingin the land wars gradually realised "Sure, they're our own people, with their potatoes, fish and children" and withdrew from further fighting against the Maori people...himselfhawk, amidst all the tur moilsofbirds, thought he heard above the din of the herd of bird, herselfs hawkwings flapping gently, arousing his passion within him but no sign of her wasto beseen only the subtle, compelling sound just beyond his senses, he was being pulled this way and that by the vision of her loveliness, his headand eyes darted, alert to her nearness but though he strained within his cage, all he could see was the madness of small winged creatures flying chaotically around a writers room, he craned his head again in full stretch as he listened closely for that ancient yet evernew call of love, she was all around yet nowhere to be seen and he fell back limp and exhausted against the side of his perch into the sleep of reason...on the bird day he rose again, Himself was not himself, whothen on the day of holy St Patrick was watching history being writ, the sin are not yet three and three for they arealso free from the not just laws and the filthgot promotion but they're nolonger doing time forbeing Irish in the wrongplace andat the wrong time, andas the train pulled into Paraparaumu McKenny was greeted by his wife and children with "your Birminghambrother is freenow after the sixteenyears" or at least that's whathim self thought heheard the North Island Robin S.M. sayas he saw her scuttleoff over the ranges and another dream of herself hadlongago been in his head before he camesouth, haere ra, e toutouwai, as his chicks came home to roost...inhis pocketis aportrait of the queen which when tumeda round fallson his head and nearly kills or concusses him itsa clean machine, he on St Padraic, the daythere of, Patrick Less no less on his way to Asia Minor spelt Myna, Kahore te ingoa; tenei manu, nakedspace behindeye, bill rather short very active and inquisitive, legs dullyellow a harsh note tells that this bird has survived anything cleared the bizzares and is now living in the relative obscurity under an uncle's tree venturing forth only to nearlyget runover by trains and boats and planes took you, aue! Iria ingoa, ignore it at your peril harbour, the war nings walking out leaving a squiggling worm fillet o' fish and finger pies in summer meanwhile back...just lieback and enjoyit and try not to think ofengland...passit out too little, but the buckstops here, out foxed buy Poontam, coon caller allblacks turngrey punchup, punchdown learn the haymaker downon the farm...Tobor cigam always has the wronganswer as metalic meta bolics age begins back wards andhim selfhawk trying to under stand it all in the confusion of what follows bytrying to understand the confusion of the past whilst livingin the con fusion of the present which he wants to giveto herselffor her birthday butshe dontlike the present without deprepence o'delord and through the door in blinding faith comes Paddymurphy crashin' the bracken crackin' like a drunken whip, "God of nations, what the fuck's goin' on here," but then hethinks "urea, I've done it," and hepisses his pantslaughing as he sitsdown at his desk a genius of a thought, "God of Nations," hewrites the first line of his hymn which has eludedhim forso long...all the smallbirds scatteras a ferocious shehawk flies screeching into the room and she wrenches with herbeak the doorof the cage which holdsher lover open, and amidst all the hoha they flee together, caught by the night aircurrents they fly on nightwings almost together like hands entwined of lovers...wingstipping they soartogether, circling higherand higher and they chant an ancient karanga through their kissing beaks . . .

the light beyond the horizon

is te Marama who,

when she shines

touches the silent, sleeping

soul of the earth

it is this unseen world

alive with the light

of the unknown

where my love for you

lies waiting

beyond those tall trees

that rising darkness

and sensuous sundown

of strange, stark colours

te po, te po, te po Aroha

the moonlight world

of our understanding

the polynesian darkness of light

the wind blows
hard out along the coast

of Parimoana

whipping up the water

scraping and shaping the land

 sending chunks of sure cliffs

 crashing to the sea below

 taurite nga moehewa o Aroha

 but now the wind has dropped

 perhaps it will wait

 then picking up my words

 Te Hau will carrythem

 soaring southwards

 over the dark hills

 taking them gently

 Kia Aroha, down the valley

 where they will reach you

 as a whisper...

at this point hawk himself realised therewas only onevoice talking, onehand clapping, it washis andshe wasgone andin the darkness, highabove the land hewept and hejust openedout hiswings and the winds blew him hitherand thither as he listlessly let the waves of sadness and aloneness wash overhim and he remembered fragmentsand fragments of fragments...beyondthose talltrees, that rising timefor beingirish in the wrongplace, whakarongo, trains and boatsand planestook you, aue! awatu! the chickens havecome hometo roast...potatoesfish and children, amodest proposal, swiftly presented for the english laughingstock crazy...and hawk himself again though he heardherself's wingsflapping gently arousing hispassion but nosignwasto be seen only the subtle compellingsound just beyond his senses...mal adjusted, just, to losingchess to his sonoutlaw e hombre this sangtara notfar from Otara butas for Tara or O'Zara (trysting dadada the nightaway)...and God's wit is spreadinga truemour from the brain about orion and mars...the winds buffeted his wings buthe held themsteady ashigh above the earth he floated northwards into the pastfuture...heyheyhawksay slowdown and the snowsdown on upokotea, whiteheadgoes onfrantic ally "fired from van Morrison - the vamp from all Irelandsite covered with smashed potatoes and pumpkin" get your whiteheadoutahere...its rifleman titipounamu, in the breastof the Southislandas kahu flies, the firstshallbe last zeezee, opzeelandia goes brownbill, whynot just pay the Bill and bedone withit e tuakana, but its not that easyeither, callmade evenmorefeeble bya twigheld...throwsa quickglass overhis shoulderat what mighthavebeen heflew soaring southwards into the past, and himself will pass eachother in the dark...c.1920 the heador rather the skullofsky, by the bucket full it was reigning catsand dogs meehoowand wolfwoof ashe waswaiting for herself andas they embraced his head wasfull of skull...believed to be or not to be Maori or polynesian twomen wereseen leaving the ho telina zephyr, westwind to you, which was laterfound ina Tautari Street, po lice were lookingfora .22 rifle, havingheard the bishop talkingthrough his mightyhat and his trans parent, I told you the bishop wasa parent hegotit from the Bi shop in K. Rd...theya fected loyalty to Caesar because they desired to have Christ declared guiltywhom they accusedof stirringup sedition, suddenly hewas grabbed around the throat and felta pistolstuck intohis back soits Jamesodonnell is itaye...in the past therewere many rebelgroups whoopposed British ruleand the treatyof Waitangi but they allgot heavily stamped on, especially when the settlers arrived toclaim theirland"...the people of the Irishrace everywhere holdin reverence the menandwomen who have foughtand bled for thecause...forhewas ethnic without beingblack, that hedid not saythe word murdered but the murd wordered...Galway and Wingatui, here Patrick begantolaugh "What's funny?" asked Paddy near the beach of tusitala Llowance for Llewellyn when hecomes running tofeelsome sympathy for the senti mentof deep in dig nation ...this ismine marktwo, blackandtan beerandstout anything goesin anything goesout, the snakewinds around both hereand a bout,...not to mention the Puckhimself when his thoughtswere in terrupted, everyone isen titled to their O'Pinions on the question of the day which for $100 is...offcourse when the language is so plane that it speaks for its elf foranin stance he had forgotten his new identity...the from dark justafter the shoneen, inside the Rosaleen Russian through his mindlike a streamofsky - the realquestion is what did the bishopin tend? Toa large ex tent this is tobe gathered from the lang uagehe used...just stones and facts welcomeas prophesised in the holy youknow what? where did youget that what...hawkhimself could feelhis flight being buffetted by the winds which meant hewas near the straight stretch between the two main islands of Aotearoa andashe braced himself for a more bumpyride he found his thoughts becoming more erratic, less comprehensible as he head ednorth, itwas as though a dream of his lives was passing before him preparing for death onlya slight erroron the Judgement Day, Rita points the bone to wards the place I've got to meether clickettyclack, I've gotta meet herclicketty clack - so the angelswere human afterall, munch munch...boomph, boomph turbulence travellingthrough the suburbs eight feet allon the back of a trailer 1 have eatendogs shit and pulled my bra and panties down outof habit the stillnessin side that littleboy isnot calmbut mena cing as the eyeofgod closes yet a gain on hum an affairs - even boats cant enter the harbour. Soa woman's secret is different to a man's even unto death she thought to himself as dusk descended on the secondday of massacre, the usual beautyof southern eveningthe evilsoul of people abstractedit self like ahid den andun seen surrealmon tage - nouse being hungryas wellas sad my love. The Banshee went totown ina brownpaper train and nevercame homea gain - I have morestories she calledback to him (shecorled baaackkktooohymnnn) and hecould hear the turalwatinaling of herbell. The object of the game is to stop others winning I cannot play he re it er ates, somehowpointing to his mangledhands, the penis raightier than the words, but both are ofcourse connected to love and words lastlonger. His head swimswithbrain awash with whiskeyonethousand miles is nota longdistance for dreams to travel (the point of misunderstanding for theanglosaxon???) herememberedhiswife (not his wife) lying likea sackof oldspuds and thinkingtohimself "Ilove her anyway" tenderly. But the reality was different for both - butitbreaksmyheartwhen I remember. The hawk realisedthat hewas dropping inaltitude andinorder to keep hisheight he wasforced to flyrather than coast, forhe was now inland...those whohaventeverbeforeseenhimarecallingandcomingcallingandcomingcallingandco ming like anancient karanga comeincomein in urgentshort burstsolhervoice and then letitstand twosisters ridingtandem well stand him rringrrringrrringis heard its stilla longway to tip, draggedout thatchroofswere torndown, earthem walls battered inby crowbards MAD (E) IN PARIMOANA and himself in the deadofsky night unseen thats the difference between a polished pig and rough diamond pickingup the pi ec es bridge of blood and gore major hokonui spillage, hukatearoa blood on the Mcahons 61/2 + 61/2 = 13 - 1 = 12 or thereabouts ifyouknow the whereabouts and have the wherewithal (if thatswhat you callsuch an insanseoreven inane collectionof quashedand puffypieces) andwith afakasi shepedals offtowards Foalalo brringbrrringrrringrrrring tingalingytingalingisathingwithouta wing some thing which existed since the beginingoftime the malooloo blew and the hawkknew te hau makariri was asign that hisjoumey was nearlyover over beenjusta dreamhis fatherhadhad, dadhadhadhadhad hahahaha dadadada dad and mummum - an aiitu riding on the backof se pasika theresnow theresno justice there's justus and he laughat the ab surdity oflanguage as a way of tryingto understand this world, this taniwha - but finally its just the darknessitself te po, te po te po nui - he hashad athought his slidingmind gradually shunting (oozingoooooozingwooooozing) out like the jampacked blackhole, sick from laughingcrying his tragic but verycatholicandirishmaori deathof superstitiouslove now the hawkis flying madlytrying toget level withwhat heseesis nowan on comingtrain a fast traincoming, birthdaybarb (50), forhe hashada vision of himself, a hawkin the snow no hues only black and whitein the night and himselfon the train thinking through the NICP of the NIMT, haurangi, hawkhas vision of death, not bloodymurder but bloodystupid falling from the traindrunk and the manhimself coke in hand woowoowoowoo trainlurches forwardback and the hawkis alongside as the dooropens ina flash of bird blinding light the himself hawk sees himself standing at the doorway train lurches back unstable on feet too much whiskey toomuch crack dangerwas in the air as the hawk who had flowna longway the wrongway in time and distance headedfor the train the light from the vestibule shining in hiseyes and he could see the startled uncomprehending drunken gaze of himself

the earth is sleeping

dreams are walking around, entering

each heart, each body

each soul is enchanted either by dreams

or nightmares haunting the darkness

with ever greater darkness

te ua, te ua, nga roimata ahau

te haunui o te wairua

te ariki kia aroha o te ao

and in the beginning was the word . . .

5

The man, himself cock in hand, in the way of his ancestors pissing it up against the wall, against it all, here he is now moving to the left, moving to the right, roving though the dark soul of the night, rocking to the rhythm of the moving train telling he cant gohome, you cant goback - clickteyclack you cantgo back - clickety clack down the track he finish his mimi, he opens the door, the train lurches forward the train lurches back himself opens the door with handle by hand a rush of cold desert nightair pushes him backwards and quickens his senses sobering him to the realisation hehad opened the wrong door, in the instant before he shuts the outside door of the train, like a vision against the whitedarkness of the snow of te Ika a Maui, its coldheart, a bird appears its hawkwing spreadopen and it seernsto fly into the vestibule of the carriage and vanish inside himself like a spirit, host of hosts, himself with himself who then has a vision he is ona train from Patras to Kalamata reading the samesign in manylanguages: ne pas se depenchen, nicht hinauslechen...e pericoloso sporgersi...do not out-bow: transfixed for that moment he senses danger and the night outside seems to call him, sohe closes the wrongdoer heopened and with a shudder he re-enters the carriage, he feels the warmth of the heater and is warmed that he is among his sleeping, talking, breathing, eating fellow-travellers as he settles down to the night's journey and the thought of herself waiting to meet him when the train arrives at the station in the morning...

END

www.ingramcontent.com/pod-product-compliance
Lightning Source LLC
Chambersburg PA
CBHW071216130626
46555CB00004B/1734